AS IT WAS

AS IT WAS

REMINISCENCES OF A SOLDIER OF THE THIRD TEXAS CAVALRY AND THE NINETEENTH LOUISIANA INFANTRY

by
Douglas John Cater

Introduction By
T. MICHAEL PARRISH

STATE HOUSE PRESS
1990

Library of Congress Cataloging-in-Publication Data

Cater, Douglas John, 1841-1931
As It Was : Reminiscences of a soldier of the Third Texas Cavalry and the
Nineteenth Louisiana Infantry / by Douglas John Cater ; introduction by
T. Michael Parrish.
p. cm.
Reprint of the 1981 ed.
Includes index.
ISBN 0-938349-47-3 : $24.95
1. Cater, Douglas John, 1841-1931. 2. United States — History — Civil War, 1861-
1865 — Personal narratives, Confederate. 3. Confederate States of America.
Army. Texas Cavalry Regiment, 3rd — Biography. 4. Confederate States of
America. Army. Louisiana Infantry. 19th — Biography. 5. Soldiers — Texas —
Biography. 6. Soldiers — Louisiana — Biography. I. Title.
E580.6 3rd.C38 1990
973.7'464'092 — dc20
[B]

90-9967

Printed in the United States of America

STATE HOUSE PRESS
P.O. Box 15247 • Austin, Texas 78761

Table of Contents

Preface		v
Acknowledgements		vii
Introduction		ix
Chapter I	Childhood	1
Chapter II	Another Move	7
Chapter III	Boyhood	10
Chapter IV	School Days—Youth	15
Chapter V	Chasing a Wildcat	21
Chapter VI	Music Lessons	27
Chapter VII	A Memorable Duck Hunt	32
Chapter VIII	A Trip to Texas on a Mule	37
Chapter IX	A Methodist Camp Meeting	47
Chapter X	My First Year of Teaching	52
Chapter XI	Teaching a Violin Class and Vacation	54
Chapter XII	New Associations and War Clouds	58
Chapter XIII	Troops Called—Becoming a Soldier	71
Chapter XIV	Off For the War	75
Chapter XV	Battle of Wilson's Creek	86
Chapter XVI	A Westward Move—Hardships and Sickness	91
Chapter XVII	Elkhorn Battle (Pea Ridge)	111
Chapter XVIII	We Cross the Mississippi I Find Brother Rufus	126
Chapter XIX	Hardships—Retreat—Sickness in Camp—Drilling	130
Chapter XX	Health Regained—Six Months in One Camp	140

Table of Contents

Chapter XXI	I Find Brother Wade's Grave Vicksburg Falls	147
Chapter XXII	Playing a Piano in the Trenches While The Enemy Charges	154
Chapter XXIII	Battle of Chicamauga — I Bury Brother Rufus	160
Chapter XXIV	Missionary Ridge Battle — General Johnston Returns	167
Chapter XXV	A Furlough and Visit With Cousins	171
Chapter XXVI	Springtime — War Renewal — Deserters Shot	176
Chapter XXVII	Retreat From Dalton — Change of Commanders — Disaster Follows	180
Chapter XXVIII	More Marching — Shoe Problems	193
Chapter XXIX	Hood Attacks — Terrible Slaughter	200
Chapter XXX	Gloom and Despair	205
Chapter XXXI	Spanish Fort — Last Battle — Surrender	208
Chapter XXXII	It is Over — Going Home	213
Chapter XXXIII	After the War — Return to Texas	223
Tribute to a General		226
Index		233

ACKNOWLEDGEMENTS

Douglas John Cater was my grandfather, friend and companion as I was growing up in Texas. During our hours together we often played checkers or chess and he shared with me his opinions, his experiences, and of course his values. Sometimes he played the piano for me, but I enjoyed most of all his performance of "Green Corn" on his old violin.

My grandfather Cater was born in 1841 in Sparta, Alabama, and grew to manhood in DeSoto Parish, Louisiana. He died in San Antonio, Texas in 1931 at the age of ninety, to the last erect in bearing, alert, and actively interested in people and events. This is his story, copied almost word for word from his own handwriting on Indian Head tablets. I remember his telling me that he carried a little pocket diary during the four years he was a soldier in the Confederate army, and occasionally he would refer to it to refresh his remarkable memory of his early life. I have made no effort to verify names, dates or places, nor to alter his decidedly critical opinions of some of the military leaders of the time, especially "The Great Emancipator." He was certainly fiercely loyal to his beloved commander, General Joseph E. Johnston.

Once I accompanied him to a gathering of old Confederates, and I well recall the chill of excitement that thrilled me when those old men stood to give the famed "Rebel Yell" of the Regiment. My grandfather's stories of the Civil War so stimulated my imagination and enlivened history for me that even today when I discover a familiar name in a magazine article or hear a reference to an event he described, I am eager to talk about those exciting days again.

I am indebted to my uncle, William Glenn Cater, for making the first typewritten copy in 1970 of the original pen and ink manuscript written by D. J. Cater. I am also deeply indebted to my cousins Robin Roberts Hagan, Barbara Cater Wilson, Lael Cater Coates, Dr. Earle David Cater, the Rev. Douglas George Cater and Margaret Cater Swarts for their help and encouragement and love, when I discussed with them my wish to preserve this record of my grandfather's adventures. It is hoped that all of you who share my delight in his style and my appreciation for the heritage he left us, will understand my great desire to publish this book in memory of my beloved grandfather, Douglas John Cater.

William D. Cater

PREFACE

Some of the experiences of the author in childhood, boyhood, youth and early manhood are related in the following pages. Not very many of them are told but enough to give the reader some information as to the difference of the environments in those years from those of the present time in our country. The schools were not free schools and parents were responsible for all expenses incurred from attendance at school. A young man who came home with his diploma was prepared for business or to take up studies in preparation for his chosen profession. He was not an accomplished football or baseball player, ready to exhibit his wonderful skill acquired during attendance at college.

Some of the author's experiences as a soldier are also related. They are copied from his diary which he kept when serving in the Army of the Confederate States of America. They may not interest those who love to read only of distinguished Generals who directed the Army movements; but young boys, noticing the little bronze cross which he sometimes wears in the left lapel of his coat, often ask him to tell them something about the war when he was a soldier. They will learn something here not found in the histories, as the historian, not being present, must get his information from others. It has been many years since these pages were written: they are fading out, and so the author has decided to have them preserved in book form with the name "As It Was."

A marble monument stands in Travis Park in the city of San Antonio, Texas. A Private Soldier with gun in hand crowns the structure. To him this little volume "As It Was" is dedicated. Chiseled on the monument base are the words "To Our Confederate Dead." Two brass cannons, specimens of the best artillery of the War Between the States, are in front of the monument and in silent words they speak, "This monument is sacred and it must be preserved." The splendid women of the South, in an organization known as "Daughters of the Confederacy" caused this memorial to be erected. Their spirit of devotion is manifest and truly is an echo of the loyalty, devotion and sacrifice of Southern women during that war.

Douglas John Cater
1841-1931

INTRODUCTION

"Three years? Yes, it is just three years today since I bid adieu to Texas friends and took up the line of march, a soldier of the Confederate States," observed Douglas Cater in a letter written from Georgia on May 7, 1864. "I was then a *twelve months* soldier, but I am now a *war* soldier. It has been three years and nearly five months since I saw my home [in Louisiana]. I was in Texas . . . and although I longed to go and say goodbye to loved ones at home, yet . . . I felt that I should go at once because my services were needed, and not wait to go home first."[1] Cater would serve another year longer, fighting in defense of the Confederacy until the end of the war.

Cater's reminiscences of his Civil War experiences, simply titled *As It Was*, comprises a superbly detailed and colorful description of a soldier's life in the ranks of the Third Texas Cavalry and the Nineteenth Louisiana Infantry. First printed by his grandson William D. Cater in 1981 in a severely limited number of copies, *As It Was* has largely escaped the attention of knowledgeable Civil War scholars and readers. Now it is available to the wide audience it deserves.

Douglas John Cater was born March 27, 1841, in Sparta, Conecuh County, Alabama. He was the third of eleven children born to William Green and Beatnah Greening Cater. An ambitious planter, William Cater

---

[1] Douglas J. Cater to Fannie Cater, May 7, 1864, Douglas J. and Rufus W. Cater Papers, Library of Congress.

moved his family in 1846 to Elysian Fields, Harrison County, Texas, but by 1848 the Caters had moved to Mansfield, De Soto Parish, Louisiana. Young Doug Cater received the finest education available in the area. He attended Keachie Institute, and then began developing his strong talent for music at Keachie Baptist College. After further musical studies under some unusually talented teachers in the vicinity, in 1859 he went to Cherokee County, Texas, where he taught music at the Female School in Rusk. In early 1861 he became head of the music department at the Masonic Institute in Henderson, Rusk County. Cater had just embarked on a promising career when the war erupted, prompting him to volunteer his services to the southern cause.[2]

In the early chapters of *As It Was* Cater describes his youthful experiences, including his family life, education, hunting and other pleasant pastimes, plantation activities and relationships with slaves, as well as social conditions. These chapters are valuable for their honest views of life in late antebellum northwestern Louisiana and northeastern Texas. Cater also recounts his musical pursuits, illuminating the essence of the elite cultural standing to which he was becoming accustomed. His family watched his progress with great pride. His older brother Rufus W. Cater commented frequently on Doug's welfare in letters written to Fannie Cater, wife of their cousin Lawrence, still living in Conecuh Coun-

---

[2] Obituary in *Confederate Veteran*, 40 (June 1932): 227.

ty, Alabama. (A large collection of prewar and wartime letters written to Fannie Cater by Rufus and Douglas is in the Library of Congress.) "Brother Doug ... [enjoys] good success as a music teacher," Rufus noted in September 1860. "He builds a pretty air castle filled with the fortune he says there is in Texas for him. It gives me no little pleasure Cousin Fannie to know that this dear young brother is successful and that he is so enterprising and so buoyant with hope. May he never know misfortune — never drink of the cup of disappointment and sorrow."[3]

Cater's stated opinions on the momentous national and local political controversies of 1860 reflect the misunderstanding and confusion so prevalent in the deep South at the time. His belief that Abraham Lincoln's so-called "Black Republican" Party intended to destroy slavery and subjugate white Southerners typifies the alarmist mentality of the period. Regardless, Cater is incorrect in his description of the chronology of the secession movement and the formation of the Confederate government. Indeed, the reader must view with great caution Cater's versions of all events in which he was not directly involved.[4]

---

[3] Rufus W. Cater to Fannie Cater, September 19, 1860, Cater Papers.

[4] For an excellent study of events in northeastern Texas during the Civil War era, see Randolph B. Campbell, *A Southern Community in Crisis: Harrison County, Texas, 1850-1880* (Austin, 1983).

In early May of 1861 a wealthy Rusk County planter, Richard H. Cumby, began recruiting a company of volunteers to serve as cavalrymen. More than one hundred men, including Doug Cater, answered the call. Representing the cream of Rusk County's young male population, they would be designated at Company B of Colonel Elkanah Greer's Third Texas Cavalry, formed the following month in Dallas.[5] "Brother Douglas is a member of the 'Henderson Guards,' a splendid company of cavalry," Rufus informed Fannie in late June. "[He] was called away without having time to come home and bid us goodbye . . . Dearly as we all love him, none of us felt that we could bid him stay when our country called him into the field." By September Rufus

---

[5] The remarkably rich and varied literature relating to the Third Texas Cavalry includes Douglas Hale, "The Third Texas Cavalry: A Socioeconomic Profile of a Confederate Regiment," *Military History of the Southwest*, 19 (Spring 1989): 1-26 [Hale also completed a full scale study of the Third Texas Cavalry, to be published in 1991]; Max S. Lale, ed., "The Boy Bugler of the Third Texas Cavalry: The A.B. Blocker Narrative," *Military History of Texas and the Southwest*, 14, no. 2 (1978): 71-92, no. 3 (1978): 147-167, no. 4 (1978): 215-227, and 15, no. 1 (1979): 21-34; Samuel B. Barron, *The Lone Star Defenders: A Chronicle of the Third Texas Cavalry, Ross' Brigade* (1908: reprint ed. Washington, 1983); Walter P. Lane, *The Adventures and Recollections of General Walter P. Lane* (1887: reprint ed. Austin, 1970). See also Joseph H. Crute, *Units of the Confederate States Army* (Midlothian, Va., 1987), 323-324.

had also caught the volunteering fever, enlisting in Colonel Benjamin L. Hodge's Nineteenth Louisiana Infantry, destined for service east of the Mississippi River.[6]

Twenty-year old Doug Cater would see his first duty as a Confederate cavalryman on the western side of the Mississippi. Because of his musical ability he served as a bugler, and he also took his violin with him to provide merriment for his comrades in camp. Yet Cater was also expected to carry a rifle and be prepared to fight whenever necessary. The Third Texas Cavalry quickly became part of Brigadier General Ben McCulloch's command, receiving orders to aid Sterling Price's Missouri militiamen in defending their home state as well as preventing a Federal invasion of northern Arkansas. Cater participated in two major battles in the Trans-Mississippi: Wilson's Creek in August 1861, and Elkhorn Tavern (Pea Ridge), where McCulloch was killed, in March 1862. He also saw action in a minor but violent engagement against Union Indian troops at Chustenahlah, Indian Territory in late December 1861.[7]

In April 1862 Price's Division (now part of Major General Earl Van Dorn's Army of the West), including the Third Texas Cavalry, crossed the Mississippi River

---

[6] Rufus W. Cater to Fannie Cater, June 26, September 20, October 6, 1861, January 19, 1862, Cater Papers; Arthur W.

[7] Hale, "Third Texas Cavalry," 1-2. Cater later wrote an article on the engagement at Chustenahlah. See D.J. Cater, "The Battle of Chustenahlah," *Confederate Veteran*, 37 (June 1930): 233.

and joined forces with the Army of Mississippi, under General P.G.T. Beauregard at Corinth, Mississippi. There Doug was reunited with his brother Rufus. "Brother Doug has endured much hardship but he is far more robust and ruddy than I expected to find him," wrote Rufus. "He has just attained his twenty-first year." Rufus seemed confident of the army's chances against Major General Henry W. Halleck's Federal forces, then threatening Corinth. "If we have anything like fair play," Rufus encouraged cousin Fannie, "you may rest assured we will send back the obnoxious hirelings of Lincolndom howling to the shelter of their iron-clad boats."[8]

But Beauregard decided to preserve his army by evacuating Corinth in late May, and the Federals withdrew to concentrate on conquering Tennessee. Beauregard camped near Tupelo, Mississippi. Here Doug made a formal request to transfer to the Nineteenth Louisiana in order to be with Rufus. His request was granted June 29, 1862, and he joined Company E as an ordinary private, forced to give up his cavalry mount.[9] "We are at present encamped in the woods in a very healthy locality," wrote Rufus. "We are required to drill four hours each day, and the strictest

---

[8] Rufus W. Cater to Fannie Cater, May 24, 1862, Cater Papers.

[9] Compiled Service Record of Douglas J. Cater, National Archives. Very little of any substance has been published on the Nineteenth Louisiana Infantry. See Ken Durham, "'Dear Rebecca': The Civil War Letters of William Edwards Paxton, 1861-1863," *Louisiana History*, 20 (Spring 1979): 169-196.

observance to duty is most rigidly exacted of both officers and men."[10]

Ordered to Alabama, the Nineteenth Louisiana served for several months as part of the Confederate garrison guarding Mobile. The regiment was now under the command of Colonel Wesley P. Winans,[11] and its close proximity to Conecuh County gave Doug the opportunity to visit cousin Lawrence and his wife Fannie.[12] "Brother Doug will visit you," Rufus wrote on August 21. "Doug was always a better boy than I," Rufus further reflected. "He has more patience and is more self sacrificing and in some respects is more charitably disposed. Don't keep him away too long. I shall miss him much." Months of inactivity at Camp Pollard near Mobile left the Cater brothers depressed and homesick. "Pollard is not very gay just now," Rufus complained in mid-March 1863. "Nothing happens to disturb our tranquility. We receive few letters . . . drill now and then for exercise, and write to all whom we love, [but] responses are exceedingly few."[13]

---

[10] Rufus W. Cater to Fannie Cater, June 22, 1862, Cater Papers.

[11] On Colonel Winans, see Ray Holder, "Col. Wesley Parker Winans, C.S.A.: A Character Profile," *Lousiana History*, 30 (Summer 1989): 279-302.

[12] Bergeron, *Guide to Louisiana Confederate Military Units*, 120-121.

[13] Rufus W. Cater to Fannie Cater, August 21, 1862, March 15, 1863, Cater Papers.

A month later, however, the regiment joined Brigadier General Daniel W. Adams' Louisiana brigade, part of General Braxton Bragg's Army of Tennessee, near Tullahoma, Tennessee.[14] The Louisianans received stirring greetings from citizens while enroute. "Many were the bouquets and verses of cheering poetry tossed to us as we hurried by the groups of fair ladies who had gathered on the road-side to see the soldiers pass as we came through Alabama and Georgia," Doug wrote to Fannie after reaching Tennessee in late April. "It is said that we are within seven miles of the enemy, but we do not know when we will fight." Rufus confessed a common fear among the troops. "The 19th La. stands a fair chance to be beaten," he admitted. "We got out of practice while at Pollard [in Alabama]. . . . Brother Doug is in good health. He sends his love to all. He is not so lively as when at Pollard but is the same good boy as then."[15]

But the Cater brothers did not get a chance to fight the Yankees in Tennessee. Instead, their regiment was soon transferred back to Mississippi, to Jackson, the capital city, where General Joseph E. Johnston's army prepared to resist the Federal corps of Major General

---

[14] Bergeron, *Guide to Confederate Military Units*, 121.

[15] Douglas J. Cater to Fannie Cater, April 30, 1863, Rufus W. Cater to Fannie Cater, May 13, 1863, Cater Papers.

William T. Sherman, part of Major General Ulysses S. Grant's army besieging Vicksburg on the Mississippi River.[16] "Heavy firing is heard in the direction of Vicks-burg nearly all the time . . . which leads one to believe that the vandals are again endeavoring to enter that city," wrote Doug on June 11. "Our soldiers have ever done their duty, but when we remember that the fate of our country will be determined by the result of this anticipated battle, each soldier will feel himself equal to three or more of the enemy, and their numbers will not frighten us."[17]

Still nervously awaiting combat on June 24, Cater expressed an increasingly uneasy feeling about the fragile character of southern morale: "I saw a gentleman who left De Soto Parish about two weeks since. He says the old men at home are all generals now — gather in groups in the little towns over there and discuss the abilities of our Generals — know more than any of them — except General Lee only. They admit him to be a great man, but all the others do wrong all

---

[16] Bergeron, *Guide to Louisiana Confederate Military Units*, 121. On the Vicksburg campaign and the subsequent siege of Jackson, see Edwin C. Bearss, *The Campaign for Vicksburg*, 3 vols. (Dayton, Ohio, 1985-1986). See also Bearss' *The Battle of Jackson, May 14, 1863 [and] The Siege of Jackson, July 10-17, 1863* (Baltimore, 1981).

[17] Douglas J. Cater to Fannie Cater, June 11, 1863, Cater Papers.

the time. Our soldiers have all come to the conclusion that they have no friends out of the army except the ladies. This seems to be really true."[18]

After the fall of Vicksburg on July 4, Sherman laid siege to Jackson for a week beginning on July 9. On the 12th the Nineteenth Louisiana was instrumental in repulsing an attack against Johnston's breastworks. But on the 17th Johnston abandoned the city.[19] "The Feds were doubtless quite surprised this morning to wake up and find no bayonets bristling over the entrenchments and no 'butternuts' to oppose their entry into Jackson," commented Cater.[20]

Soon afterward the regiment joined the Army of Tennessee, now commanded by Braxton Bragg.[21] At Chickamauga, in northern Georgia, on September 19 and 20, Bragg won a hard fought tactical victory, but the Nineteenth Louisiana lost almost half its numbers in casualties. Here Rufus Cater was killed. At Missionary Ridge on November 25, during the Chattanooga campaign in southern Tennessee, Bragg proved his in-

---

[18] *Ibid.*, June 24, 1863.

[19] Bergeron, *Guide to Louisiana Confederate Units*, 221.

[20] Douglas J. Cater to Fannie Cater, July 24, 1863, Cater Papers.

[21] On the Army of Tennessee, see Thomas Lawrence Connelly, *Autumn of Glory: The Army of Tennessee, 1862-1865* (Baton Rouge, 1971). See also Richard M. McMurry, *Two Great Rebel Armies: An Essay in Confederate Military History* (Chapel Hill, 1989).

capacity as a field commander by losing a strongly defended position to Grant's repeated assaults. Colonel Winans was killed, and Colonel Richard W. Turner, took command of the Nineteenth Louisiana.[22] "It is true cousin Fannie, we have been out generaled and defeated but we must not despair," wrote Cater. "There is more dissatisfaction among our troops now than there has been at any time before this. I am pained to see it. . . . Many have deserted because they were denied the furlough promised them when they were conscripted and retained in the service. . . . We are not, we will not be whipped. Liberty and independence must be, will be ours."[23]

In late December Johnston replaced Bragg as commander of the Army of Tennessee. His primary responsibility was to defend Georgia against Sherman's invasion in the spring of 1864.[24] Cater and his comrades

---

[22] Crute, *Units of the Confederate States Army*, 152; Bergeron, *Guide to Louisiana Confederate Military Units*, 120-121.

[23] Douglas J. Cater to Fannie Cater, December 21, 1863, Cater Papers.

[24] Sherman's invasion of Georgia and the crucial Atlanta campaign receive thorough, if not altogether original, treatment in James Lee McDonough and James Pickett Jones, *War So Terrible: Sherman and Atlanta* (New York, 1987). For a superb guide to the literature on the subject, see Stephen Davis' and Richard M. McMurry's "A Reader's Guide to the Atlanta Campaign," in J. Britt McCarley, *The Atlanta Campaign: A Civil War Driving Tour of Atlanta-Area Battlefields* (Atlanta, 1989).

welcomed Johnston's arrival with almost unanimous approval and satisfaction. "I am proud to see this spirit of reanimation taking place," Cater noted while in winter quarters near Dalton, Georgia. "I hope it will insure success to our cause and liberty and independence to our nation. It will show the world as well as our enemies that we are not yet whipped nor subjugated." By March he seemed even more enthusiastic. "Our troops all have more confidence now than at anytime during the past 5 months," he asserted.[25]

During May of 1864 the Nineteenth Louisiana saw action in a series of battles near Dalton, serving in Brigadier General Randall L. Gibson's brigade. Johnston then withdrew to a position north of Atlanta.[26] "The army continues [to be] in good spirits," Cater wrote on June 24. "There have been some desertions in the army—mostly Georgians whose homes have been lately left in the Yankee lines. Let them go—if they are not for us,let them be against us. We would rather fight them than feed them." But by July 4 Cater began doubting Johnston's ability to save Atlanta. "He has a brave, cheerful and hopeful army," wrote Cater,

---

[25] Douglas J. Cater to Fannie Cater, January 19, March 11, 1864, Cater Papers.

[26] Bergeron, *Guide to Louisiana Confederate Military Units,* 121.

"but it is not large enough to drive Sherman out of Georgia."[27]

President Jefferson Davis, believing that Johnston would make no effort at all to defend Atlanta, replaced him in mid-July with General John Bell Hood.[28] "The change does not meet the approbation of the soldiers generally," Cater commented to Fannie, "but . . . Hood will do us the best he can, and it is evident that under him we will have to fight." Soon afterward, at Ezra Church on July 28, the Nineteenth Louisiana saw the harshest combat of the campaign. "Our Brigade made an unsuccessful charge on yesterday," wrote Cater. "We were not supported properly . . . and the result was we were repulsed with heavy loss. Our regiment went into the charge with about 200 men and lost more than half of their numbers in killed, wounded and missing. . . . The regiment is always unlucky in an engagement and suffers a severe loss. I have reason to be thankful that my life is still spared."[29]

---

[27] Douglas J. Cater to Fannie Cater, June 24, July 4, 1864, Cater Papers.

[28] On Hood, see Richard M. McMurry, *John Bell Hood and the War for Southern Independence* (Lexington, Ky., 1982)

[29] Douglas J. Cater to Fannie Cater, July 26, July 29, 1864, Cater Papers.

Stationed in the defensive works outside Atlanta, Cater informed Fannie on August 4, "Yesterday we were listening to a sermon when we had to leave the minister in the midst of his discourse to take our places in the trenches, expecting an attack. We have prayer meetings every night when it is quiet enough to allow it. The troops of our Brigade, not withstanding their late losses, are in good spirits and sanguine of success, although I fear I notice a change in the other Brigades of our Division. It is now believed that General Hood will not give up Atlanta and many Yankees as well as Southrons will find their last resting place in front of Atlanta before Sherman enters the city a victor."[30]

True to Cater's prediction, Hood offered stubborn resistance but finally evacuated Atlanta on September 1, giving Sherman a monumental victory that sealed the North's resolve to win the war. Hood then decided to march northward in a desperate effort to distract Sherman and dislodge Federal occupation forces in Tennessee. On November 30, at Franklin, Hood sent his troops forward in a suicidal attack against the enemy's formidable breastworks.[31] Fortunately for Cater, the Nineteenth Louisiana did not arrive on the field in time to participate in the slaughter,[32] but described the

---

[30] *Ibid.*, August 4, 1864.

[31] On Hood's Tennessee campaign and his costly assault at Franklin, see James Lee McDonough and Thomas Lawrence Connelly, *Five Tragic Hours: The Battle of Franklin* (Knoxville, 1983).

[32] Bergeron, *Guide to Louisiana Confederate Military Units*, 122.

aftermath in a letter to Fannie. "I went over a part of the battlefield the next morning," he wrote. "The ditch in front of the enemy's works was filled with dead, dying and wounded Confederates, many of whom had received bayonet wounds which showed that there had been a hand to hand fight. . . . They were lying with their scarred faces upturned amidst heaps of Federals. . . . Those of the enemy who were captured told us that we could go anywhere, even to New York, if we attempted to march with the same determination as that with the battle of Franklin was fought."[33]

Despite the debacle at Franklin, Hood forced the Federals to withdraw to Nashville. There they won an overwhelming victory on December 15 and 16. The shattered Army of Tennessee then broke up. The Nineteenth Louisiana was sent to Mobile, where it fortified the city's garrison in a forlorn attempt to resist a Federal siege during late March and early April of 1865.[34] Cater surrendered along with the rest of his fellow Louisianans soon afterward. On May 16 he wrote to his cousin Lawrence, "I am ashamed of many of the people of the South, i.e., the male population. . . A few brave men were left in the field to meet the enemy while at least two thirds of the men who could fight had become tired and quit. Such men do not deserve freedom. . . . Whether or not I made a good soldier is not for me to say, but I have done my duty in

---

[33] Douglas J. Cater to Fannie Cater, December 15, 1864, Cater Papers.

[34] Bergeron, *Guide to Louisiana Confederate Military Units*, 122.

every capacity ... and now I believe that I can make a good citizen. At least I am willing to share the fate of my friends in the seceded states."But he qualified this statement of resignation with a sharp comment: "I am anxious to get on soil not occupied by the enemy. I think I can *breathe easier*. There is no love in my soul for Yankees, neither can there ever be."[35]

Cater's observations in *As It Was* regarding the trials of Reconstruction reflect his continuing animosity toward Yankees, especially the black Union troops that arrived in northwestern Louisiana immediately after the war. Attempting to resume a normal life, he took up the study of medicine but later engaged in farming. Yet music always remained the great interest of his life. In 1866 he married Emily Mary Reagan of Rusk County, Texas. Three sons were born, but they, along with his wife, died within ten years. Cater then moved to Lovelady, Texas, and in 1880 he married Belle Barbee. They had a daughter and four sons. Cater became a Postmaster at Lovelady and also served four years as Treasurer of Houston County. He was a Mason and a member of the Baptist Church as well as an active participant in the Albert Sidney Johnston Camp (Number 144) of the United Confederate Veterans. After moving to San Antonio, he died suddenly in his home on November 23, 1931, at ninety years of age. Cater was buried in Roselawn Cemetery. His wife, daughter, two

---

[35] Douglas J. Cater to Lawrence Cater, May 16, 1865, Cater Papers.

sons and their wives were also buried there. One son was buried in the Confederate Cemetery in San Antonio, and the last son, Glenn Cater, died in Austin in 1989. Several grandchildren and great grandchildren carry on the Cater name. An obituary article in the June 1932 issue of the *Confederate Veteran* magazine concluded with a fitting tribute to Cater: "A man of noble purposes, ever loyal to all that was good and true, was D.J. Cater."[36]

T. Michael Parrish
Austin, Texas

---

[36] This information on Cater's postwar life was supplied by his grandson, William D. Cater. See also the obituary in *Confederate Veteran*, 40 (June 1932): 227.

CHAPTER I

CHILDHOOD

One of my earliest recollections was of a time my brother Wade and I were playing at a spring of clear, cool water which gushed out of the base of a little hill on my father's plantation in southern Alabama. An empty flour barrel with both ends open had been placed in an excavation in the soft sandy earth around the spring, holding the water which had been let in and which had come bubbling up from the bottom of this improvised basin; whence it could be used for all necessary farm and household purposes. When full to overflowing the water passed out through a 'V' shaped notch in a stave of the barrel: thus beginning a clear running stream that flowed through the plantation. We were very small boys and were trying to sink a gourd in the spring. Some of the Negroes had given us the gourd and told us we could not sink it if we did not cut a hole in it and let it get full of water. We were soon convinced that they were correct. We then cut a hole in the handle and held it under the water until it was full and then turned it loose and it sank to the bottom of the spring where we had to leave it. We decided to ask our father to tell us why we could not sink the gourd without letting water into it. When we told him about it, we also told him of throwing rocks and some pieces of iron into the spring which sank at once. He said there was no air in the rocks and iron but there was air in the gourd and when we grew older he would tell us how the air got into the gourd before we cut a hole in it. He also said that if we threw any more rocks or iron into the spring we would wish that we had found some other place to play.

I went to school one day with brother Rufus and sister Victoria. Brother Rufus was four years older and sister Vic two years older than I. My brother Wade was two years younger. Mr. Wesley Brown was the teacher. He had noticed that I was soon very tired of school, and after the noon recess he told me to take a nap on a bench in the school room. I tried to sleep and was very glad in the evening when I heard him say, "School is dismissed." He went home with us that evening and stayed all night. Next morning, after breakfast, he said to me, "Young man, are you going with us today?" I answered, "No sir, I got tired yesterday and was too glad to get home last night to want to go any more."

I remember that not very long after that day's school experience I was very sick. It was with very great difficulty that I could breathe. The night seemed so long as I watched my mother and father sitting at my bedside, sometimes rubbing my throat and chest with a kind of liniment and giving me medicine which the doctor had left for me to take. They were bathing my forehead and temples with a warm wet cloth and would leave it there for a time and then they would take it off to be wet again in warm water and replaced. When I could breathe easier, I would go to sleep, soon to be awakened by a struggle to get my breath.

One day while we were playing a game of marbles in the smooth, sandy, clean-swept yard in the shade of a huge oak tree, my father said to us that he was going to take us way out to Texas. Of course we had never heard of Texas, and our surprise and regret were very great that we were to leave this pretty home forever. We wished that there wasn't any Texas.

Not long afterwards we were on a railroad train speeding toward Montgomery, Alabama. We were going faster than I had ever ridden, and as the railroad coaches filled with people my wonder was very great. I watched the movements of this, a flying machine to me, as we rapidly passed the trees and farms and houses near the railroad track. Nobody in the coaches seemed to be afraid and the people would walk in the little aisle between the rows of seats while the train was moving. All this was new and wonderful to me.

We went from Montgomery to Mobile. At Mobile we were placed on a steamboat to cross Lake Pontchartrain en route to New Orleans. This steamboat was another wonder and surprise to me. I watched with intense interest the great wheels on the sides of this steamboat, plowing through the water, and I thought of the little flutter wheels brother Rufus had made for me and brother Wade, and had placed in the running branches after a heavy rain. I remembered the gourd brother Wade and I could not sink in the spring at the old plantation as together we stood and watched the onward movement of this great steamboat carrying so many people without sinking. We concluded that it must have been made out of some material like the gourd that we could not sink. As we looked at the people walking about on the boat with perfect ease, we ceased to be afraid and even felt safe. We looked out upon the large body of water on which we were riding, with no land in sight, and watched the many large white birds flying and following close to the boat, unmolested by the people.

Arriving at New Orleans we left the boat and were taken in an omnibus to the St. Charles Hotel, where father said a short stay would be necessary because we would have to wait for a steamboat which would be ready in a few days to take us to Shreveport. While at the hotel we heard may people talking about Texas and Indians. Brother Wade, although two years younger, was large as I, and much braver. Upon hearing those people talk about Texas and Indians, Wade said, "I wish we could hurry on, I want to see an Indian." But I felt I would rather be back at the old home in Alabama playing marbles under the old oak tree in the yard, or watching the Negroes plowing or picking cotton. Of course we did not like the city, as everything was so different from the country. We missed the quiet farm life where we did not see so many people hurrying on the streets and sidewalks, all strangers to us.

In a few days we were again on a steamboat, en route for Shreveport, Louisiana. We were on the waters of the great Mississippi River, steering north. Arriving at the mouth of the Red River we left the Mississippi and continued north on the muddy waters of the Red. It was much smaller, and the steamboat we were on had no side wheels, but had a wheel at the rear of the boat. It did not move as fast as the boat on the lake, which had carried us to New Orleans. Sometimes when it was winding its way around the bends in the river it looked like it was going to strike the bank of the river. It did stop several times, but the stops were to take on more people who were also going to Shreveport on their way to Texas. After some days and nights on that boat we arrived at Shreveport. This was a small town but it was of much importance in those days because it was a shipping point. Many boxes and barrels were taken from our boat and were carried to the stores in town on drays, which were large two wheel carts drawn by mules. The merchants were waiting to receive the goods. Many bales of cotton were piled near the river awaiting shipment. Much of that cotton had been hauled many miles from the farms in Texas and some of it had been sold to buyers in town and some was to be shipped to New Orleans before being sold.

Our stay in Shreveport was short and we were soon on the road in wagons, bound westward for Texas. Father had brought our Negroes and some wagons and teams and provisions necessary for the trip. At the end of the day's journey a camp was arranged, and after supper we were soon asleep on blankets and quilts for beds on the ground; to be awakened early the next morning to get ready for another day's journey. We continued on until we arrived at Elysian Fields in Harrison County, Texas, our point of destination. But this part of Texas was not a wilderness and brother Wade's desire to see an Indian was never realized. The Indians had all left for new hunting grounds farther west in Texas. Large plantations were in cultivation. Crops of corn and cotton were growing, promising an abundant yield; other crops, and gardens of all kinds of vegetables were growing, and orchards of peach trees were laden with delicious peaches. Fig trees were heavy with fruit, and all showed a land of plenty. School houses, which served also for places of worship, as well as other community gatherings, in different parts of the county, were evidences of prosperity, and an enterprising people.

Uncle Edwin Cater, my father's oldest brother, lived there, and of course this was one of the influences which caused my father to move to Texas. Shreveport was the nearest market for cotton, where it could be sold or shipped to New Orleans.

This was in the year 1847, and I was six years old. Brother Rufus and sister Vic attended school with two of Uncle Edwin's children, Tom and Martha. His youngest daughter Kate and I were of the same age and too young to be sent to school, so we and brother Wade were playmates at home, since the families lived near each other.

CHAPTER II

ANOTHER MOVE

My mother's sisters and one of her brothers lived in DeSoto Parish, Louisiana, and Mother, desiring to live near them, persuaded my father to buy unimproved land near where they were living. So after being only one year in Texas, we made another journey with wagons and teams and Negroes, camping out at night on this move, as we did on our trip from Shreveport out to Texas.

The land which Father bought was situated three miles southwest from Mansfield, Louisiana. There was a log cabin and thirteen acres of cleared land on the tract, but the balance of the land was wild and heavily timbered and much work had to be done. I was too young to do anything except get in the way sometimes while watching the Negroes at work.

Saw mills were few and a long distance from our place, and for a time planks or sawed boards were the only lumber used for the doors, windows, shutters and floors for the new houses. To make troughs in which to feed the stock, Father would select a large pine tree, as near all heart as he could find, have it cut down with a cross-cut saw, and sawed into the length he wanted the troughs. Then he would have the heart burned out, which was done by applying fire to the end of the log. When it was sufficiently kindled, all the trash or rubbish was taken away, leaving the heart of the log burning, which in a few days would be burnt out, leaving the log hollow. This was then split into halves with a maul and wedge, making two troughs. Pieces of plank were nailed across the ends and the trough was complete. I remember spoiling two intended troughs by throwing chips to see the sparks fly from the fire inside the burning log. I was passing it about dusk on my way home from the field, when I saw the fire burning slowly, and the trouble started. I did not know the damage I was doing. After I went away the chips burned causing a blaze and the next morning as I was passing the log on my way to where the Negroes were at work, I noticed that it had burned off where I threw the chips at the fire. When Father saw it he knew that some one had thrown something on the fire inside. I heard him ask, "Who did it?" I knew I needed punishment, but I decided it would be safer for me not to tell him that I did it. I did tell him about it much later, and my reasons for not telling him when he was trying to find out who spoiled his troughs. He only laughed and said he had forgotten about it.

I attended my first school in this neighborhood and received my first lessons in Webster's blue back speller. A Mr. Tom Hendricks was the teacher. He was a small ugly man, but I liked him. It took me some time to distinguish the letters b, d and p, but Mr. Hendricks had patience with me. I finally learned one from the other and after this I learned to spell, and then to read. The school sessions were not long, but I was always glad when Saturday or vacations came. Brother Wade and I enjoyed them about the farm or in the woods.

As we grew larger the hook and line and little fish in the creeks had attractions for us. Returning home one day about noon with a string of nice fish, we passed a spring in the field and stopped to get a drink of water. This spring was not a fast gusher, but boiled gently from the ground in a little branch. A keg or half barrel with the ends out had been placed there to hold the water, and thus make a basin for it. When full, the water would run out over the top. A gourd to drink out of was kept there, but on this occasion someone had taken the gourd away and had also taken out several buckets full of water thus lowering it about a foot from the top of the keg. We did not wait for the spring to get full, but thought we could rest our hands on the edge of the keg and safely drink from the spring. Brother Wade made a successful effort and got a drink, but my hands slipped and my head went to the bottom. I could not get my feet down because the keg was too small and I was getting decidedly more water than I needed. Brother Wade, with a strong effort, pulled me up to my feet to where I could get my hands to the edge of the keg and this helped me to get out. The water had filled my ears, nose and mouth, and for a few minutes I suffered from being strangled. When I recovered fully we went home. My mother's cook, Aunt Becky, dressed and fried our fish for us for dinner, although she had already prepared dinner for the family. We often talked of our experience of that day, which made us more careful about drinking water like 'Gideon's rejected warriors,' when we were away from home.

CHAPTER III

BOYHOOD

By the time I was ten years old, Wade and I had learned the use of a gun. There was a rifle in our home, but in those days there were no cartridges and the rifle was difficult to load. Father moulded lead balls for us and gave us a powder horn and taught us how to use them. In loading the rifle it was necessary to fill the charger with powder and pour it into the rifle barrel, then place a piece of thin cotton cloth over the muzzle of the rifle and put a ball on it and press the ball down until even with the end of the barrel. With a sharp knife we then cut the cloth off which was outside the muzzle and pressed the ball down with the ramrod of the rifle until it rested on the powder. It was necessary for the ball to fit firmly in its place. The ramrod was then returned to its place on the outside of the barrel; a cap was put on the tube and the gun was ready for use. This slow and difficult process of loading made us very careful of our aim in shooting and we seldom failed to bring down the game we shot at. Later Father bought a single barrel shotgun for us which was not so much trouble to load, and was not so heavy to carry as the rifle. We used a powder measure or charger for it also, which held more powder than the rifle charger. We would fill it with powder and pour it into the empty gun and then place a little wad of paper, which was rammed down into the barrel and pressed firmly on the powder. Next we filled the same charger with small shot and poured them into the barrel and placed another wad of paper which was pressed down firmly on the shot. The ramrod was put in its place and a cup put on the tube and our shotgun was ready for use. This could be done quicker than loading the rifle and on this account we quit using the rifle. We carried home squirrels, quail and doves in abundance. Game was plentiful. When we saw a squirrel in a tree one of us would remain with the gun on one side of the tree and the other would go to the opposite side. This was generally sufficient to make the squirrel go to the side of the tree where the boy with the gun was waiting, but if not sufficient, the other boy would make a noise or shake a bush or throw a stick. If this failed and the squirrel decided to leave that tree and seek safety in another, we would follow and watch for another opportunity to get a shot at it. If the squirrel should succeed in getting to a tree which had a hole either in the main body or in a limb of the tree, that squirrel would be safe from all hunters and we would have to leave it in the "security of its retreat."

My father was a good rider on horseback and an expert with a shotgun in hunting deer with dogs. He kept two and sometimes three hounds and often hunted deer with them. When I was large enough to ride and guide a horse he bought a saddle for me and I sometimes went hunting with him. I soon learned much of the woods and would sometimes do the driving. This was to take the dogs with me and go into the woods where there were deer, and Father would go to a 'stand,' which meant a place where the deer would be apt to run across a road when pursued by dogs. We each carried a blowing horn which was tied with a string and swung around our necks and usually under the left arm so as to be secure and yet not in the way when we were either mounting or dismounting. When making the drive in the woods I would blow my horn occasionally to let him know where I was. He taught me the signals made with the horn. These signals were used by hunters and were as follows. One sound was, "Where are you?" answered in the same way meant "Here." Two consecutive sounds, "I want you to come to me," four sounds in succession, "I have killed a deer and need your help." Our irregular sounds of the horn were 'calling the dogs.'

Our dogs were very industrious and without any encouragement from me would hunt faithfully every scope of woods through which I rode. When they found the trail of a deer they would bark occasionally, but did not go fast, and I could stay near them easily while they were following the trail. The deer would be sometimes asleep or sometimes grazing, but when the dogs got near them they would run and then the race commenced. I would stay with the dogs, or as near them as I could, by making my horse run through the woods, bushes and trees, and by jumping over logs or fallen trees until I arrived at the place where Father had gone to take his 'stand' to wait for the deer to come out of the woods.

Sometimes he would take a stand in the woods where the deer were in the habit of passing when not pursued by dogs and hunters. Often he would kill the deer there and a further race would not be necessary. But if the deer was wounded we would together follow the dogs through the woods until they caught it. Sometimes the race would be a long one and in this way I soon became a good rider and could carry my gun while on the horse.

One cool morning in October, when I was twelve years old, Father told me to load my gun with nine buckshot and go to a place where we had frequently seen deer cross the road. I was to tie my horse and take a stand about thirty yards in front of him. This was where I could see him, so as not to shoot him if I got a shot at a deer. He had not forgotten that Mrs. Campbell of Mansfield had shot at and killed a deer which was passing between her and her horse, and had killed her horse also with the same shot. He said he would make a drive and that he believed he would run a big buck out to me. I obeyed his instructions and did not have to wait long after I took my stand before I heard the dogs 'in full cry' coming toward me. On they came, and I could feel and hear my heart pounding from excitement and expectation. Soon I heard the deer bounding toward the tree in front of which I was standing. There were some bushes not far in front of me, and while waiting for the deer to pass them and come out into an open place, I got ready to shoot.

Soon it came, a large buck with heavy horns, but as he emerged from the bushes he saw me and made a quick turn, making a high leap as he passed a pine tree. I fired but he ran faster and was soon out of sight. The dogs were following not far behind him, and upon hearing me shoot, increased their speed.

Pretty soon Father came galloping up and asked,

"Hello son, where is your buck? I saw him and he is a fine one, and when I heard you shoot I expected the dogs would stop, but they went on." I replied, "I expected to kill him but he went faster after I shot at him." Father then said, "Let us look around a little; we will find some blood if you hit him." Dismounting, he went to where I said the deer was when I shot. The pine tree was about thirty yards from where I stood.

When he looked at the tree he smiled and said, "Son, how many shots did you have in your gun? I see you hit this tree." I told him that I had loaded my gun with nine 'blue whistlers.' He said, "We will count those in the tree: here is one, two, three, four, five, six, seven, eight, nine, and they are higher than my horse. They are all here; no use in looking for blood, and no use sending you to a stand if this is the way you shoot!" I really could not account for the reason I missed the buck, but remembering that he made a high jump when passing the tree as I fired, I said, "I had a good aim on him, but that pine got in the way just as I shot. I know I shall have better luck next time I get a chance to shoot at a deer." Father replied, "I hope so, and I will try to give you another chance before long."

CHAPTER IV

SCHOOL DAYS – YOUTH

As was mentioned before, Mansfield was our nearest town and was three miles from our home. There were good schools in Mansfield, one for boys and one for girls. After the little country school near our home was discontinued and Mr. Hendricks, our teacher, had returned to his farm, Father sent us children to school at Mansfield. The walk was long and we had to get an early start from home to be present when school opened in the morning. There was no time for loitering on the road, and in the evening when school was dismissed, no time was to be lost if we were to get home before dark. When the weather was bad and rainy we could not go.

On Saturdays there was time for play and brother Wade and I used it in many ways. Father gave the Negroes holiday in the afternoon and we often spent it playing with the Negro boys. We sometimes would take axes with us and one of our pastimes was to let a Negro boy climb a sapling and we would cut it down just to see him jump out when it was falling. None of them ever got hurt and they liked the sport.

In the autumn we would go with some of the Negro men opossum hunting at night. They loved to go with us, and they liked the meat of the opossum when it was well cooked. Sweet potatoes cooked with it added much to its flavor. We were not afraid of getting lost if one of the Negro men went with us.

Our dogs could hunt coons and opossums at night as well as they would hunt deer in the daytime. They learned the folly of running deer at night because they received no reward for it, but they seemed to enjoy a race after a coon. If they could compel the coon to go up into a tree, the dogs seemed to know that the Negroes with axes would come and cut the tree down and thus dislodge the coon so they could catch it. They manifested much impatience while waiting for the tree to be cut down.

One night they forced a coon to go into a tree which was so large that the Negroes decided there was too much hard work necessary to cut the tree down for just one coon. I had my gun with me and I told them we could build a good fire and wait until morning when I could see the coon well enough to shoot it. They agreed to this proposition and we carried it out, but it was not agreeable with my father who was very uneasy about us when we remained in the woods all night. He forbade any more hunts at night during that winter.

Foot racing during the noon recess at school was one of the pastimes enjoyed by the boys. I pulled off my shoes and socks one day to make a race with a fast running boy of my age. This was wrong because my feet were very tender. About midway in the race, when I was ahead and felt sure I would win the race, I stepped on an upturned sharp piece of dried and well seasoned weed. The weed penetrated my foot and passed through it between the first and second toe bones, pushing up the skin on top of my foot and breaking off. This caused great pain and I could not walk. My feet were tender because I had not commenced going barefooted that early after winter.

I was carried into the schoolroom and placed on a bench. The teacher sent a runner for a doctor who came and examined the damage and said he would have to do some cutting to make an orifice large enough to insert an instrument with which to pull the weed out. When he commenced cutting I asked him to give me some chloroform so that the pain caused by cutting into my foot would not be so great. But he objected to that and continued his cutting. I was afraid I could not endure the pain inflicted by the cutting, but he positively refused to grant my request. When the opening was large enough, he inserted a pair of forceps and pulled out the weed. It was hard as a piece of wood but when it was taken out and the pressure against the bones was relieved, the pain ceased.

I thought and still think I was treated cruelly in not being allowed something to help me bear the pain caused by cutting into my flesh. Of course, I was glad when the ordeal was passed and the pain gone. The doctor's name was Godfrey. He carried me home in his buggy and even carried me in his arms into the house. My mother was frightened when she saw him lift me out of the buggy, but he explained the situation and told her I would be all right in a few days. This proved to be true and it was not very long before I was at school again, but not ready for a foot race.

I must tell of one Fourth of July celebration in those

happy, carefree days. The people of Grand Cane and vicinity, seven miles from our home, celebrated an anniversary of the Declaration of Independence with a picnic and barbecue. Brother Rufus, then a lad of sixteen summers, and John Garrett a young school teacher of that neighborhood, were the orators on that occasion. They were both familiar with the history of the American Revolution, as well as the speeches of great men who were foremost in severing the American colonies from the control of Great Britain. Brother Rufus and Professor Garrett acquitted themselves with honor, receiving rounds of applause and manifestations of approval at the conclusion of their speeches, and were the honored guests at the superb dinner which followed.

I was much interested in the preparations for that dinner. On the day before, a long ditch three feet wide and two or more feet deep was dug and logs of green hickory wood burnt into coals. The burning coals were spread evenly on the bottom of that ditch and the carcasses of dressed hogs, sheep, goats and young oxen were put on sticks placed transversely across the ditch, and were cooked slowly over the burning coals until nearly noon on the morning of the Fourth. New burning coals had to be put under the meat occasionally. When it had been thoroughly seasoned with salt, pepper and vinegar while over the fire and had been pronounced 'cooked enough' by the chief manager, it was taken to a long table and nicely carved, after which it was taken to be served on the tables.

These tables, in a large square, enclosed the carving

table. Baskets, boxes and trunks were filled to overflowing with bread. Cakes, pies and pickles had been
prepared by the good women and girls of the neighborhood to be added to the barbecued meats. Large iron
pots of boiling coffee inside the enclosure were ready
to be dipped with tin cups, and the coffee passed to
those who enjoyed that beverage, at the conclusion of
the speeches. I tipped my hat to Brother Rufus as he
and Professor Garrett passed me, escorted by a bevy of
pretty girls on their way to the dinner table.

After this sumptuous repast, there was music and
dancing and different plays at the residence of Mr. Lee,
near the area of the barbecue. The large house and the
large yard were full of merry people, young as well as
old. The sun was sinking behind the western hills
before all of these patriotic denizens of the Grand Cane
neighborhood had dispersed for their homes.

When I was fourteen years old my father obtained a
mail contract for me to carry the mail on horseback
once a week, about twenty miles, from Mansfield to
Logansport, Louisiana, a town on the Sabine River, at
the state line between Texas and Louisiana. The trip
was to be made in one day.

I was never in love with this job. It was a long
lonesome ride, both going and returning, and I had to
start very early and lose no time, or else be in the night
getting home. I had often heard of mail robbers and on
some of my lonesome rides I felt like I ought to have
some kind of a weapon to defend myself, but no one
ever molested me in any way.

On one trip I failed to deliver the mail at Logansport

because of the high water. A large slough in the swamp near Castor Bayou, across which the road passed, was filled with back water from the bayou which was overflowed with heavy rains. This slough had been dry where the road crossed it and I knew its depth. I knew my horse would have to swim to get across. Logansport was only five miles distant, but I turned back towards Mansfield. I had not learned to swim and I felt safer out of the water.

The Postmaster said I ought to have delivered the mail to Logansport wet or dry, but my judgement was decidedly against what he said, and my father said I did exactly right; that I must not take any foolish risks. Some horses swim like a deer with only the head above water, but others can swim shallow enough to prevent their riders from getting wet if they will keep their feet up in the saddle. I didn't know then how my horse swam but I knew I was not going to force him into that slough!

CHAPTER V

CHASING A WILDCAT

Uncle John Greening, one of my mother's brothers, who lived at Pleasant Hill, not very far from his plantation on Red River, paid us a visit during the autumn of 1854 and was so well pleased with our home that he made my father a flattering offer for the place. This offer was accepted and a sale was made, which of course made another move necessary.

I loved this home with its long associations and I was sad when told that Uncle John was now the owner; and I wished that he had not paid us that visit. The only consolation to me was that when we moved away I would be rid of that once a week trip I had to make from Mansfield to Logansport with that mail bag across my saddle.

The new move was made, and in January of 1855 we were in another home sixteen miles north from Mansfield on the Shreveport road, and five miles east of Keachie, a small town in the northwest part of De-Soto Parish. Mr. A. Conway of Macon, Georgia, was the owner of this place and had brought a number of Negroes to be put on the plantation. He was a tailor by profession, and knew nothing about farming, and was not yet ready to leave Georgia. He and Father entered into a three year contract, Father to take charge of the plantation and cultivate it with his own and Mr.

Conway's Negroes. Mr. Conway was to furnish as many mules and wagons as Father.

This was a very large plantation and here brother Wade and I received our first lessons in the use of the plow and hoe. We learned how to use both but were not kept steady at work. We learned how to swim in the waters of the bayou that coursed its way through the western side of the plantation. We also hunted and fished, but paid very little attention to our books, except sometimes to read; and we had many experiences.

It was during this year that I got rid of the asthma which always made me sick and annoyed me every time I took a cold. This cure was made by taking pine rosin pulverized and mixed with honey. The rosin was taken from a cut or bruised place on the pine tree where the gum had oozed out and formed lumps, becoming very hard and brittle when exposed to the air and sunshine. It was easily pulverized and when mixed with honey was not a bad medicine to take. A tablespoon of the mixture taken frequently during the day and sometimes at night, relieved me from an affliction that often annoyed me and caused suffering, as far back as I could remember.

One morning while the dew was on the grass and bushes, brother Wade and I had an exciting race with the dogs after a catamount, or wildcat. We were barefooted but got along pretty well through the bushes and the grass, which was over knee high and wet with dew. We had heard the dogs running before we got out of bed. We started just after daylight, and of course before breakfast, to go to them. The cat had sought safety in a tree by the time we got to the dogs. My gun was loaded with squirrel shot which were too small to have much effect on so large an animal, except at short range. It leaped from the tree when I fired the first shot, but it was only wounded and soon went up into another tree. My next shot was a little nearer and it fell out of the tree. It put up a hard fight and the dogs were badly bitten and scratched before they succeeded in killing it.

Another time we were squirrel hunting in a swamp. Seeing smoke not far from us, brother Wade suggested that we investigate the cause of the smoke. We found the camp of a runaway Negro man. There was a frying pan with several slabs of bacon well cooked on some coals of fire, a little bag of corn meal, two tin plates, a knife and fork and a tin cup, a blanket on a bed of dry leaves. All had been hurriedly left, and we decided that it was better and safer for us to leave this camp just as we found it. We knew that the Negro was watching us from behind a log or tree not far away and if he attempted to fight us we would have to shoot him, and we did not want to hurt anybody.

We went home and reported our find to Father, who said, "Perhaps the Negro felt that he had been mistreated by the overseer, and decided to quit work for a while in revenge, knowing that he would or could get something to eat from the other Negroes at his home as long as he stayed in the woods." But his being there made brother Wade and I select other hunting grounds for a few days. We were at that place afterwards, but there was nothing to interfere with our hunt.

Our move from the old home near Mansfield to the

place where we were then living caused my mother's seamstress much anxiety and sorrow because her husband belonged to another man and she was twenty-five miles from her husband. My father, seeing her distress, told her that he would make an effort to buy Joe (her husband) and that he would send me with enough money to induce Joe's master to let us have him. Somehow Father believed that I could make a better plea for Joe than he could, and said he believed I would bring Joe home with me. Joe was a good man and very valuable and his owner did not like to give him up for any consideration. But he, too, was a good and tender hearted man and finally yielded to my pleadings, and consented to let me have Joe for $1,100. Joe went home with me and I noticed that there were no dry eyes at the conclusion of that transaction. Sarah gave me a long hug when she saw that Joe was with me when I got back home, and Sarah and Joe were not the only people there who were glad and happy.

This is a quite different version from Harriet Beecher Stowe's novel *Uncle Tom's Cabin*. I imagine her husband told her that if she expected to make any money with her novel she must put it strong, and Harriet did 'put it strong.'

The next year Father bought an open top one horse buggy and said brother Wade and I must use old Tom, my mother's buggy horse, to go to school. He told us to take sister Vic with us. She was older and he said he could trust her to take care of us.

There were two schools at Keachie, one for boys and the other for girls. The girl's school was on the west side and the boys school was on the east side of the village. As sister had to attend the school on the west side and brother Wade and I on the east side, this made an extra mile for Tom, and a very early start from home was necessary.

Brother Rufus attended our school but boarded in town. In addition to his studies, he taught some of the classes.

After school was opened in the morning, the spelling class was called first and immediately afterwards the grammar class. Brother Wade and I were in both these classes, and these lessons had to be learned at night at home. The drive was long and so much was to be seen along the road, both going and returning, that there was no time for studying these lessons except at night.

Uncle Bob, a favorite old Negro man, took charge of Tom when we got home in the evening about sundown, and had him hitched to the buggy and ready for us the next morning as soon as we had eaten breakfast. Our attendance at these schools with Tom and the buggy continued for two years.

Those were happy days and it is always with sweet recollections that I recall them. But the two years did not terminate our school days at Keachie. They fulfilled Father's contract with Mr. Conway who decided to leave Georgia and move to his plantation in Louisiana. Father bought another home about four miles southeast from Keachie. After we moved to the new home, it was decided that Tom and the buggy should be left at home and that brother Wade and I, being larger now, must walk to school.

The Baptist Association of North Louisiana took charge of the female school and made a college out of it. Large and suitable buildings were erected and a president and necessary teachers employed. Sister Vic boarded in the college. Brother Rufus continued his studies and teaching in the male school. But he had a spell of measles which injured his eyes to such an extent that he was compelled to discontinue both studies and teaching.

He went to Milton, Florida, and sold goods for a time for cousin Lawrence Cater, a merchant. His eyes got worse and he went to New Orleans and had them treated, but received no benefit from the treatment there. He then returned home. This condition continued until and after he entered the Confederate States Army.

CHAPTER VI

MUSIC LESSONS

Miss Ella Taylor of Polk County, Texas was employed to teach music in the new college. Sister Vic and I took music lessons from Miss Ella. Brother Rufus and sister Vic had attended a singing school at Grand Cane, where we lived near Mansfield, taught by a Dr. Willis, who had given up the practice of medicine for a while and taught vocal music. I joined them at home in their practice and learned the scales and the songs they practiced. Dr. Willis used "Mason's Sacred Harp" as his textbook. It was published in round notes. The first few pages contained lessons on the staff and clefs, the different kinds of time, and the necessity for the flats and sharps used in music. In fact, it was a grammar of music and the information I gathered from that old "Sacred Harp" was of much value to me in learning piano music. My father was much pleased with my success in learning to sing with the others who attended Dr. Willis's singing class at Grand Cane. He manifested this during a protracted meeting at that place not long after Dr. Willis taught there by asking me to lead the song service one afternoon.

The people carried dinner and had forenoon and afternoon services but no night preaching. I was much surprised, and so were the people, when Father asked me to lead the singing, but I had learned obedience, and without making excuses or apologies, did as he asked.

I think my singing gave satisfaction because I had to help in the music at every service after that, and often as leader. This additional study and its necessary practice at the piano, and the long walk going and returning from school left me no time for idleness or games at play.

I sometimes took a deer hunt on Saturdays with Father. My experience on the morning I shot the pine tree instead of the buck, was worth much to me and I very seldom missed a deer when an opportunity came to shoot at one, and in our hunts, I killed as many deer as Father did.

I killed a large buck on Saturday in the drive and when I blew my horn I expected Father to come to me. Pretty soon I heard him galloping past me, not paying any attention to me nor to the call I had made with my horn. I did not understand this, and mounting my horse, I soon overtook him. I hailed him and told him I had killed a big buck in the drive. He said, "I know it, but don't you hear Volsey Rambin's dogs coming? They will run a deer across the Mansfield Road a quarter of a mile from here and I want to get a shot at it." "All right," I said, "I hear them now and am sorry I halted you."

He went on and I went back to my buck to wait for him. My stopping him caused his failure to get to the road soon enough. He saw the deer but it was too far from him to shoot it. When he came back to me I told him again I was sorry that I had been so impatient, but he said, "Don't worry about it, my son, of course you didn't know why I passed you in a run; it doesn't make any difference, we have a fine buck and that is enough for this day's hunt."

I had not taken music lessons very long before Miss Ella Taylor, my teacher, was prostrated with an attack of typhoid fever, and was sick many long weeks and died. This was sad for us all, pupils, teachers and other people. Miss Ella was a splendid character, a beautiful woman and a Christian.

This death caused a vacancy which had to be filled and the Board of Trustees employed Miss Fanny Thomas, a lady from New York City, for the remainder of the session. She resigned before the end of that session. I never knew the cause of this resignation. Miss Isabella McCormick from the same state, New York, was then employed as Music Teacher. She loved violin music and asked me to bring my violin to the music room and practice some pieces with her, which she said we would play together at the closing exercises of the school term.

There were no graduates that term, but it was to be closed with recitations by pupils of both schools. Essays were read by both boys and girls and speeches made by the boys. In those days people were not looking forward to the time when their girls would become public speakers. The higher advanced girls were required to write and to read an essay at the college commencements. The boys were taught oratory, and on this occasion they were required to 'declaim' or make speeches. They had committed to memory some of the famous orations of public men and could and did declaim them to an appreciative audience. My music teacher varied these exercises with piano and violin music. She at the piano, and I with violin, played several pieces and received applause. Miss Fannie Wells, one of the music pupils, and I, sang a burlesque courtship and dialogue which drew more applause and favorable comment than any of the other exercises.

Miss Isabella was not with us after that session. She captured old Ratt Crosby, a rich widower who had attended the school closing exercises. His given name was Erastus, but he was called "Ratt" for short. Old Ratt had a very long hook shaped nose and gray hair and was considerably stooped when walking. After listening to Miss Isabella's music and getting acquainted with her, his lonesome home was more lonesome than ever. Miss Isabella, having an eye to business, decided that he was neither old nor ugly and that a home with him was much more to be preferred than the daily listening to youngsters count one, two, three at the piano. A wedding followed and we lost Miss Isabella as a teacher. Miss Sallie Carlton of Shreveport was employed to fill the vacancy, but I did not take lessons from Miss Sallie.

Professor Roy, a graduate in music from Germany, was teaching a class in Kingston School in DeSoto Parish. His class in school was not large enough to require all his time. He bought a horse and saddle and spent two days of the week on a circuit, giving music lessons, and I met him at one of his appointments. This was at the home of Mr. Tom Hall whose two daughters took lessons, and I made the third pupil at this appointment. It was seven miles from my home. I rode on horseback twice a week to Mr. Hall's to get instructions from this German music master; a fourteen mile ride to receive an hour's teaching. He was thorough in the science of music and a good instructor. My ambition then was to secure a profession and be a master in music, and I studied and practiced faithfully. With this entry into the study of music with Professor Roy, my school days at Keachie ended.

CHAPTER VII

A MEMORABLE DUCK HUNT

I continued to take music lessons under instructions of Professor Roy during the remainder of that year and all of the next year until July 1859.

In January of 1859, Frank Greening, a son of my mother's oldest brother, Dr. Wade Greening of Milton, Florida, was a visitor at our home and asked my parents if brother Wade and I could go with him on a duck hunt to the lakes northwest of Mansfield. These lakes were about twenty miles east from where we lived. My parents consented for us to go with Frank and we started on horseback soon after dinner on this long ride, carrying blankets, cooking utensils, guns, ammunition, something to eat and corn for our horses.

We were tired when we arrived at the lakes at about sunset. Our first work was to water our horses and feed them. Next, to prepare a place to sleep and then cook supper. We found wood in abundance for a fire and sufficient dry leaves to make a good bed after our blankets were spread over them. The winter had come and there were no snakes crawling around, nor scorpions in the leaves to make us afraid. The alligators had gone into their winter retreats and the outlook for a hunt was good, but soon after we had lain down in front of a comfortable fire for a night's rest, talking of our plans for the next day's hunt, rain commenced falling gently.

The weather was cloudy but we had heard no thunder and were not expecting rain. The rain was sufficient to force us to move our camp. It was a fine dry weather camp but there was no protection against rain. Somebody had built a shelter for camping purposes, when either fishing or hunting on the lake, and it was only 200 yards from our camp, but we had not thought that we would find a use for it. Leaving the horses we moved to the shelter. We again arranged our blankets for a bed, but there were no dry leaves under this shelter, and our sleeping place was not warm. The rain soon quit falling, but there now was loud thunder and fierce lightning for a time and then a cold north wind came. The shelter afforded no protection against wind and there was little sleep for us. So, huddling around a little fire which the cold wind almost put out, we passed the remainder of the night. We could not return to our first camp because the ground and leaves were wet. This was a very long night.

The clouds disappeared during the night and the wind ceased its terrific blasts, but continued to blow from the north. We were sleepy before daylight came but were ready, having eaten breakfast and fed our horses, when the ducks started flying over us. We commenced shooting at them but with poor success. We soon learned that if we could not see their eyes when they were flying over us that they were too far away.

Leaving what ducks we had killed at the camp, we went near the water's edge and took a jaunt down the lake. We had not gone far before I shot a duck which fell about forty yards out in the lake. I thought we ought to leave it because we had neither a dog nor a boat, but Frank was so anxious to get it that he proposed we go after it as it was a fine one. He said we could take off our clothes and wade out to it. He said he would go with me if I would lead the way. We did as he suggested and found the water only a little over waist deep, so we did not have to swim, but the water was very cold.

After we got back on land I told him that I would not go in the water after any more ducks; that the water was not only too cold to take that kind of risk, but we might step into an alligator hole. The lake was full of alligators in the summertime and they were now in these holes, and I did not want to get in company with them. He said, "All right, but we will have to be careful and shoot so that our ducks will not fall into the water." We put our clothes and shoes on and again started down the lake.

We had gone but a short distance when a canoe in good condition was found tied to a sapling at the edge of the water. We got into it and had no more trouble about getting our ducks out of the water. We rowed about 200 yards from the land and found a little mound of solid earth about five feet in width and length and about a foot above the surface of the water. I stepped out on it and finding firm footing, I asked brother Wade and Frank to leave me there a little while and make a circuit toward our camp and they would be apt to send some ducks by me. But after they left me the wind commenced blowing hard, and having to stand in one place without exercise, I soon got cold. They returned in about two hours or perhaps not so long a time, but I was so cold I could hardly get into the canoe. We picked up the ducks I had killed while they were gone and rowed hurriedly to our camp.

It was then about noon. Brother Wade soon had a cup of hot coffee for me and that together with a good dinner soon warmed me up, and I was ready for another jaunt. But we agreed after dinner that it would be better to go home than to stay out another night, as we had plenty of ducks from one hunt.

It was after dark when we arrived at home and we were a tired trio of boys. A Negro man took charge of our horses and not long after supper we were in bed and asleep. The next morning I discovered that I had taken cold and in fact I was quite sick. Pneumonia developed the next day, and Father sent for Dr. Rochelle. His first treatment was a fly blister applied to my breast. Then followed other medicines. It was several weeks before I was well enough to leave my bed. I was apparently well, but painful boils which had to be lanced, came in succession one after another on my breast, where the fly blister had been applied, and they continued until the following summer, leaving scars I am yet carrying.

Brother Wade was taken sick a few days after pneumonia developed in my case. Dr. Rochelle treated him in the same way that he had treated me. His fever was higher and he was delirious, but after a few days a discharge from one of his ears showed that an ear drum had broken, which had been the cause of his fever and delirium. This began to leave him and he became rational. Calling for a small mirror, he looked at his blistered breast and said. "This is the first time I ever heard of a man being blistered on the breast for an earache!" This remark caused quite a laugh from those around his bedside, as he was only a youth, but the doctor was firm in his convictions and declared he had made no mistake and that our sickness was caused from cold contracted in our deer hunt. Frank Greening was more fortunate. He said the outing had benefitted him. This experience, of course, put an end to our hunting for that winter.

When I recovered from this attack of pneumonia, I resumed my study and practice of music with Professor Roy. At the close of the school term at Kingston, the latter part of June, he gave a concert. All of his pupils took active part in this concert. It was while attending the closing exercises at the Kingston school that Professor Roy told me that it was not necessary for me to continue taking music lessons because I was prepared to teach music and ought to secure a class somewhere when the schools opened in September. I had made good use of my time devoted to the study and practice of piano music under his instruction. I appreciated his statement that I was prepared to teach, and said that I would act on his suggestion after taking a little vacation to look for a place where my services might be needed.

CHAPTER VIII

A TRIP TO TEXAS ON A MULE

Sam Adams of Lavaca County, Texas, was on a visit to his brother Elisha Adams, a near neighbor of ours, and was about ready to start on his return home. Tom Adams, also a neighbor, but not a relative of Elisha Adams, had a brother near Huntsville in Walker County, Texas. He decided to visit that brother and start in company with Sam for a part of the journey. E. B. (Ned) Adams, a son of my father's sister Leah, lived in Polk County, Texas, and Sam Adams proposed to Father that I go with him and Tom that far, on Sam's return home, and make a visit to Cousin Ned. 'Boy like,' I wanted to make the trip as these men would be good company and I really wanted to see some of Texas. Jim, the only idle mule on the place, was the only chance for a mount for me. He had been bought out of a drove of mules two years before, and at first positively refused to let anyone ride him. I had seen him throw a Negro man, a good rider, seven times in succession one day before the man could stay on him, and I hesitated before I agreed to make the trip on him. He had quit trying to throw anyone off his back, and rather than give up this opportunity to see some of Texas, I accepted Jim. He was faithful and I made a good hunting mule of him before my return from Texas. Dismounting, I could drop the bridle reins on the ground and leave him and he would remain where I had left him.

Instead of going through Polk County as had been

promised, a different route was selected after we started. We crossed the Sabine River at Pulaski, and went through Panola, Rusk, Cherokee and Houston Counties together; but after passing through the town of Crockett in Houston County, Sam bade me and Tom good-bye, going westward, and Tom and I turned south. We passed Nevil's Prairie, the first prairie I had ever seen. It covered an area of about twelve square miles. There were herds of cattle on it and we passed two little farms. We stopped at the first one of these to get dinner. There were several men at this place on the same errand. One of them took a fancy to Jim and tried to persuade me to swap Jim for his horse, a good looking animal and a fine saddle horse, according to his owner. "Nothing doing," I knew Jim but I didn't know this horse nor his owner. We stopped for the night at the second farm. It was just out of the swamp of the Trinity River bottom. The next morning our road led through the swamp and across the river at Wiser's Ferry.

We arrived at Huntsville about noon and decided to inspect the Penitentiary. The manager was kind and showed us every part of it: the cells where the prisoners slept, the shops and looms where these prisoners worked, making shoes and cloth. We saw them stand in line at dinner time while they were searched for concealed knives or weapons of any kind before marching to dinner. We passed one dark cell in the building where we were not allowed to talk nor whisper near the cell because the inmate was in solitary confinement for life, for the crime of murder. This was my first visit to a prison of any kind. I learned there what a penitentiary was in reality, and I thought, "Oh! How much happier men would be and how much better would be the condition of all people if they would not disobey nor violate the laws of our country!"

Tom Adams' brother was manager of W.O. Baldwin's plantation south of Huntsville, so after our penitentiary visit, we went to his house and stayed all night. This was the place to which Tom Adams had started when he left home, but I had yet a journey of forty miles ahead of me before getting to the place I had left home to visit. Polk County was east from Huntsville and Cousin Ned's home was four miles from Moscow, a village in that county, so when asking directions for my route I called for Moscow. This part of my trip was alone with only Jim for company. Tom Adams said he would remain a week with his brother and then come by Cousin Ned's for me when he started back home.

I stopped at Waverly in the evening. This was a nice looking little town and it seemed to be inhabited by people of culture and wealth. At any rate I decided to seek lodging there for a night. I applied at a pretty residence. The 'man of the house' looked at me in surprise, as the situation seemed novel to him, but he agreed to let me stay. His name was Lewis and I found that I had stopped with a family of refined people. There was a good piano in the parlor and there were some young ladies in this family who made good use of that piano after supper. It must have seemed odd to them to have for a guest a traveller whose mount was a mule, and I could not tell whether they played for their own amusement or my entertainment. But after they had seemingly tired of their music, one of them ventured to where I was sitting and asked me if I could play.

The question, of course, was to draw me into conversation. In those times, as a rule, boys did not have piano music among their other lessons. I answered "Yes" and she said, "Please play some for us!" I had been out on the road more than a week and was a little afraid of making a blunder in playing from memory. My hands, too, were getting pretty hard from exposure and rough usage, but from the expressions on the faces of these young ladies after my first piece I knew that my effort was not a failure. The first touches of the keys brought the whole family into the parlor. Mr. Lewis, the father of these young ladies, after listening to several pieces said, "We have a music teacher employed for the next session, otherwise we would make you a proposition."

I then told him that I had taken music teaching for my profession and although I had not taught any, I expected to commence somewhere when the fall sessions of the schools opened. He then talked more freely, and after learning where I lived, said he had an old Alabama neighbor and friend living near my home, in the person of Captain Y. W. Graves, and gave me a message for him. The evening passed very pleasantly and by bedtime I was pretty well acquainted with the family. When I was ready to start on my journey the next morning, I asked him how much I owed him for taking care of me the past night. He answered, "Not a cent except a promise to come to see me if you are ever in this part of Texas again. I am glad you spent the night with us and I want you to come again. Don't forget my message to Captain Graves."

I arrived at Moscow after a long lonesome ride, but I was still four miles from Cousin Ned's and had to get directions to find his home. I arrived there about dark. I had seen him at our home and knew him, but of course had to tell him who I was. He and his family gave me a hearty welcome. He told a Negro man to take charge of Jim and give him water and a good supper by himself where the other stock could not bother him.

A week passed quickly, but during that week we had several deer hunts and I killed three deer. One of them was a very large buck with velvet still on his horns. Bob Lockhart, Cousin Ned's son-in-law, but whose wife was dead, was making his home with Cousin Ned. Bob proposed a drive the next evening. There was an extra shotgun in the house and I used it.

In the first drive, Bob shot at a deer but missed it, and it came out of drive by me. I had not arrived at the place at which I was to take a stand, and so had not dismounted, but Jim stopped and I took the risk of shooting from the saddle and killed the deer.

The next evening another hunt was proposed. A large buck had been spending the nights on the plantation but particularly in a pea patch and had become so fat that he was careless about leaving the plantation, and slept in the daytime in a scope of woods where there was much underbrush and bushes. Cousin Ned said that he believed we could get him and told me where to go and take a stand. He said that he and Bob would take the dogs and go into the plantation and that he would make a drive through that scope of woods, and Bob could take a stand at another place where the deer had been coming over the fence. I went to where I was directed, and I had not dismounted when I saw the deer which had heard Cousin Ned's horn and decided to leave that scope of woods at once. Coming within about sixty yards of me he stopped. His body was behind a large tree and I could see only his head and a part of his neck. I took aim at his head which was crowned with a pair of heavy horns, and I fired. He ran on but made a turn towards the fence, leaping it easily when he got to it and was out of sight before I could get another shot.

I heard the dogs coming then. They had come to the place where he had been aroused by the sound of that horn. I rode forward to the place where he had leaped the fence and saw blood on the top rail. I dismounted and waited 'till the dogs came up and helped the ones that could not climb over the fence. I stayed pretty close to them until a heavy shower of rain and thunder and lightning stopped me. I could not hear the dogs after the rain commenced, so I dismounted, and taking my saddle blanket, wrapped it around me and stood against a tree, the heavy leaves of which made a shelter until they got thoroughly wet, when I had to move. When the shower was over, arranging my saddle I mounted Jim and rode forward in the direction I heard the dogs before the rain. I had not gone very far before I saw one of them standing very still and looking toward the ground. I rode up to where it was and found the deer which was dead.

The other dogs quit the race when the rain commenced falling. One shot had cut the deer's throat and it had bled to death. I sounded my horn for help but nobody heard me; I had gotten too far away. I remembered crossing a dim road just before the rain and set out to find it. I didn't feel like I was lost but I didn't know where I was. I found the dim road but after following it probably a mile it ended and I was still in the woods. I knew if I would go back on the same road it would take me out of this wilderness because it had been used for hauling logs. I had to hurry because the day was nearly gone. This part of Polk County was sparsely settled and the country was comparatively new. This road led by Cousin Ned's plantation to his house. He and Bob had not come home but the little boys Dood and Frank were there and when I told them I had killed a big buck and had to leave him, they said, "We will go back with you and get him." They saddled an extra horse and it was not long until we were tugging at that deer to get him into my saddle. We tied it with a plow line in the saddle and I rode behind the saddle. We went slowly but got home safely with our buck before dark.

Pretty soon Cousin Ned and Bob got home, and Dood said to them, "You are nice fellows deserting one of your crowd in time of need." They answered that they had heard me shout and had heard the dogs run off and concluded that I had followed the dogs. They had blown their horns 'till they were tired, and as all of the dogs except one had come to them, they finally concluded that the missing dog was with me. Thinking that if I had not been driven home by the rain, they would hunt for me and that the dog might aid them in finding me. They expressed pleasure at finding me safe at home, but seemed even more pleased when they saw the 'peafield buck' which Dood said, "Us boys had killed."

I went with the family to Moscow on Sunday to hear a sermon by the pastor of the Baptist Church there. Before church services I met Cousin Ned's widowed sister Mrs. Catherine Womack and her daughter Nellie, a young lady of sixteen summers. I also noticed a fine looking man at the services whose hair was tinged with gray and whose eyes were not on the preacher, much over half the time, but often over in our direction. I was sitting with Cousins Catherine and Nellie, and after the sermon, I called their attention to the man who looked more at us than at the preacher, and Cousin Catherine said, "That is Foster Poe, an old bachelor who lives near the village." Nellie said, "Cousin Doug, I believe that old fellow is going to be my step papa; Mama calls him old Foster but she likes him." I learned afterwards that Nellie was correct. Her mother married old Foster (as she called him) a few months after I was with them at that church service.

A day or so after this, Tom Adams and his brother William, who decided to go home with him, came to cousin Ned's and asked for me. Tom said he had promised me to come by after me when he started home, and was making that promise good. Cousin Ned told them they must stay all night as I was out somewhere and would not return before night.

The next morning I bade good-bye to this family with whom I had spent such a pleasant week, and set out for Keachie, Louisiana. Tom and his brother were good company, but we were all tired by the time we got home on the fourth day after leaving Polk County. On our first day's journey it was nine o'clock at night before we found a shelter for the night. This was in the southern part of Angelina County which in those times was lonesome. We might have stopped early in the evening but we wanted to travel 'till nearly sundown. When that time came no house was to be seen and we rode many miles before arriving at a field or house of any kind. The people who lived in the house where we stopped had taken in some travellers before we got there, and 'twas bedtime with them. The good people of this home told us that were it not a fact that the next house on the road was several miles distant we could not stop with them. We thanked them and told them that if they would let us have something to give our horses to eat we could do without eating, and would sleep on the gallery until the next morning. They would not agree to this proposition, but said we must have something to eat after the long ride. They soon had prepared a really good warm supper, which we enjoyed after feeding our horses.

We got an early start the next morning and made a forty mile journey in time to stop before night. This took us nearly across Nacogdoches County. We stopped long enough in the town of Nacogdoches to visit the noted old stone fort there. This old fort had been built for a place of refuge from Indians and

Mexican raids in the earlier history of this part of Texas. When we visited the old fort we found a man in it, selling whiskey by the drink, as well as by the bottle and jug. Our crowd was temperate and our visit was to see the fort and not to buy whiskey. The next day's journey was across Shelby County to Logansport on the Louisiana side of the Sabine River. The last day's ride was not so long. Sixteen miles on the Shreveport road brought us to Keachie. Here I parted from my travelling companions, the Adams brothers, and went home four miles out. My father and mother were beginning to feel like they would like to know what had become of me and Jim. They said they had not been uneasy about me, but were glad I was at home again. I had not written to them, but in a few days I had given a full account of my trip. Brothers Rufus and Wade said they would have enjoyed some part of the trip, but the long tiresome rides would have taken away all the pleasure.

CHAPTER IX

A METHODIST CAMP MEETING

School days as a pupil were over, but I found out afterwards that I ought to have been given at least two more years in the literary department at Keachie School before beginning to teach music. I was eighteen years old in March, 1859, but an ambrotype taken that year at Mansfield shows more boy than man.

Joe Williams and his sister Margarette, young friends who lived near us, had just returned from their visit to relatives living in Rusk in Cherokee County, Texas. They said a music teacher was needed in the high school at Rusk, and they had told their relatives that if I had not been employed somewhere else, they might secure me. Professor John B. Mitchell of Virginia, was the superintendent of the school. I wrote to him for information in reference to the matter. His answer was that the session would open the first week in September, and that if I wanted the music class, to let him know. I did so and promised to be with him on time. I was now to bid adieu to Father, Mother and my brothers and sisters, who all seemed nearer and dearer to me than ever before, and begin work in my chosen profession. 'Twas too late to be a coward and I must go forward. The last week in August Father said he would take me to Rusk in his buggy, and we set out on the long journey. At Keachie Father asked Mr. Spilker, who had a store of confectioneries, bottled wines, etc., to put a bottle of good brandy with our lunch in a pair of saddle bags we had in the buggy.

We decided to go by way of Elysian Fields in Harrison County and spend the night there at a Methodist camp meeting, where we could hear some good preaching. We found a great many people there and some from Keachie, who had preceded us. This was the first camp meeting I had ever attended. The tents were arranged in good order extending in a square around a large brush arbor where religious services were held. Pine straw had been gathered and hauled there in wagons and spread on the ground under the arbor and the tents, to be used as a carpet. The seats under the arbor were long rough benches arranged so as to seat 2,000 or more people. Scaffolds, five or six feet high, covered with planks, and the planks covered with sand or dirt, had been built at the sides and ends of the arbor, and at night pine knot fires were built on these scaffolds to give good light. The night scene was pretty, and the impressive services made me feel like I was on sacred ground.

I had heard Negro women shout under the influence of religious songs at their places of worship, and in those days the Negroes made music all its own, none other like it; but here at this camp meeting was the first time I had ever heard white women shout. The shouting commenced when prayer was offered for those who had an invitation, went forward and knelt at the benches in front of the improvised rostrum, to be prayed for. The space between these benches and the rostrum was called the 'altar.' Those persons in the audience, who had relatives or special friends kneeling at those benches, were requested to come to the altar and kneel by them and pray with and for them. The loud and earnest prayer of the preacher touched the hearts of those Christian women who were kneeling in the altar and their shouts and hallelujahs were heard a long distance away.

I confess a peculiar indescribable sensation came over me when listening to those shouts and I had no comments to make; but certainly had very great respect for those ladies engaged in this part of the service. The Satanic Majesty had made his way into this camp meeting and was putting in some of his best work. Some young people were sitting on the bench immediately in front of Father and me. One young lady said to another, sitting by her, "Let's go up there and shout some." The other agreed to it and they started for the altar. Dick Hollingsworth, from Keachie, was sitting near us. He whispered to us that he was going to follow and go on the outside of the arbor and watch to see if those young ladies carried out what they had proposed to do. Dick returned in a few minutes and told us that they were both shouting at the altar. It will not do for me to express my opinions here. I will say, however, that if they believed that good would result from what they did, it were better that they had not said what they were going to do before leaving their seats. It seemed to me that this was evidence that the Devil was taking a hand in this camp meeting.

On our arrival at that camp ground, some friends who knew my father, asked us to spend the night with them in their tent. We accepted the invitation and after caring for our horses, put our baggage and saddle bags in the tent. After supper we went with these friends to the arbor. After the services at the arbor were over, we returned and slept the balance of the night in the tent. We were up early the next morning to get ready for the long drive before us on our journey to Rusk. After breakfast with our good friends, they asked us to take a lunch with us for noon, but we told them we had a lunch with us in our saddle bags and after thanking them for the kind offer, and giving us a nice place to sleep in their tent, we bade them good-bye.

About twelve o'clock we stopped near a creek where we could get water for ourselves and our horses. Under the shade of a large oak tree, we sat down on the grass and Father said, "Now for dinner." But there wasn't any dinner. While we were at the services under the arbor at the camp ground, someone had entered the tent and robbed our saddle bags. Our dinner was gone and with it our bottle of brandy. We didn't care much for the loss of the brandy, as it was only to be used in emergencies, but we needed the dinner. So this was added evidence that good people were not the only kind who attend camp meetings.

We drove another mile and stopped at a farm house near the road, where we obtained dinner. We were on the road for several days. Arriving at Rusk we stopped for the night at the Thompson Hotel. Next morning we called at the home of Professor Mitchell and introduced ourselves. The professor manifested some surprise at my youthful appearance. Nothing had been said about my age in our correspondence. He said I would get a good class of piano pupils.

The second morning after our arrival at Rusk, Father said good-bye and started on his long lonesome journey for home. I don't know how he felt, but it flashed over me about the severed home ties and about the strangeness of my situation. With everybody a stranger, and all faces new, I could not help feeling lonely and sad. Having looked to my father from my earliest recollection for everything, with never a care on my mind, I felt that I was not yet prepared to face life's duties alone. But I knew now that I must henceforth depend more on myself and accustom myself to my environments. In other words, I must 'paddle my own canoe,' and live up to my conceptions of right in everything. I knew too, that there was work ahead of me, and my resolution was to do my duty.

With these thoughts I returned to the hotel and made arrangements for a room and board. I found it necessary to rent a piano and then ascertain who would patronize the music department to be added to the school. I desired also to secure the names of the pupils who would take music lessons. When I was introduced to Dr. C. B. Rains, whose daughters were among my pupils, he said, "Why sir, I expected to see a man and you are nothing but a boy!" I replied to him that I only asked a trial. This reply seemed to impress him favorably and he then said, "You shall have my daughters for pupils."

CHAPTER X

MY FIRST YEAR OF TEACHING

Four months passed rapidly and the Christmas holidays came, and with them a desire to see the folks at home. Professor Mitchell said this desire came very soon, but offered no objections. I went on the stagecoach to Marshall and from there to Shreveport on the train; and then on the mail coach from Shreveport to Keachie. A week at home passed quickly, and when the time arrived for me to start back to Rusk, the home folks said they had hardly seen me. Some of the Negroes at home had saved a watermelon for a Christmas present for me. They had preserved it in good condition from the fall crop of melons. I don't know how they did it, but the melon was certainly a 'nice treat.'

After leaving home I spent a pleasant evening at Shreveport with Misses Tempie and Emma Alston. They were childhood playmates at the first school I ever attended. Their parents lived near my home and I was frequently with them when there was no school. They called to mind, many little pastimes on the old playground, some of which I had forgotten, but these now young ladies easily called them to memory.

On my return to Rusk I found the young people were continuing the rounds of parties and social gatherings. I attended some of them before resuming my duties in the school room and felt that I was benefitted. I met and associated with young men and women of the town outside of the schools. I had not made their acquaintance before, and I didn't feel so much like a stranger among them afterwards.

Time passed rapidly and my first year's teaching was drawing to a close. Then the people and the patrons would desire to know of the progress of the music pupils. A concert was necessary; in other words, a musical entertainment. I had never given a concert and my only experience in this line was the part I took in Professor Roy's musical entertainment at Kingston, and Miss Isabella McCormick's part in the closing exercises of the first session of the Keachie College. So I decided not to waste time in rehearsals but let my pupils continue their lessons and simply let them show their progress by playing and singing some of the pieces they had learned under my instructions. When the time came, I made out a list of what I wanted them to play and sing. Our exercises were to close the school for that term. I gave the list to Professor Mitchell and asked him to open the exercises with any kind of speech he thought best to make, and then call out the names of the pupils, and the names of the pieces they were to play in the regular order. As each one finished her piece and when they had all played, he was to call on me for a piece and this would conclude the exercises for the evening. This program was carried out fully and the rounds of applause following each performance showed appreciation. I was congratulated as having given a satisfactory showing of the session's work and an entertaining concert.

CHAPTER XI

TEACHING A VIOLIN CLASS AND VACATION

Vacation had come and I was ready to start home when I was offered one hundred dollars to teach a class of violin pupils at Alto, Texas, for one month. I accepted the offer as I would still have one month for vacation after the end of the violin school. I had never given lessons on the violin, but I had learned to play that instrument when a small boy. The Alto people who had attended our entertainment believed I would make a success with a violin class and were willing to risk a hundred dollars on a trial. Their faith made me try the harder not to disappoint them. A month's lessons would give a pupil a good foundation and by earnest application afterwards he could learn to play without a teacher.

I had a blackboard made and we commenced the lessons. The first one was a bedlam. Fifteen violins in the hands of men and boys, no two making the same sound and all starting at once trying to play a scale I had written on the blackboard proved that I would have to make a decided change from the way we had mapped out. I taught them how to hold the violin and the bow, and at the blackboard explained the alphabet of music; made the ladder with its whole and half steps to show them what was meant by the term scale; all of which they could understand. I told them our first effort had taught us an important lesson and that was, that each one must be taught separately and alone if we expected to make any progress. So I arranged to give each one an hour's lesson every other day, which would be eight hour's work for me one day, and seven hour's work the next.

Professor Tinnon, a dancing master, taught a class in dancing at the hotel where I was boarding the same month in Alto. After my work hours I spent some time, at his request, in his dancing room, watching and sometimes practicing with his class. I was not one of his pupils but I learned to dance the cotillions, reels, schottisches and polkas, and I learned to waltz. It was recreation for me and Professor Tinnon had asked me to exercise with his class. I could play all of his pieces on the violin and he said he really enjoyed having me practice with his pupils.

The end of the month came. I had complied with my contract with my violin class and was ready and had determined to take vacation the next month. Some of the pupils had made good progress, but there were some of them who did not practice and the only attention they gave the violin was when they were taking a lesson or listening to somebody else play. I bade my pupils and friends at Alto good-bye and started for DeSoto Parish, Louisiana. The weather was very hot and the ride before me long and lonesome. But Sir Robin, my horse, was a good traveller; in fact, the best saddle horse I had ever ridden. He had no other redeeming traits. He was a vicious animal and never made friends with me, although I took good care of him and gave him only kind treatment. I had to watch him and never allow him any advantage of me. If an opportunity came he would kick me if I attempted to mount him from his right side.

I must tell of witnessing a strange sight one day while at Alto. A man by the name of Mathis, who was hauling lumber with a team of four yokes, unhitched or unloosened the wagon tongue from the first yoke but did not unhitch any of the others, and drove them into a lot to give them water in a trough from a well forty feet deep. The top curb of this well extended about four feet above the ground. This curb had decayed at the surface of the ground but was still in place. One yoke of oxen ran around this curb to get to the trough and the chain which linked them to the next yoke caught around the well curb and jerked it away from the well. This caused one ox to fall into the well; his weight drew his mate in; this added more weight and the next yoke was drawn in. This continued until six oxen were in the well. The fourth yoke of oxen were at the well's mouth when the first ox reached the bottom, but the well was full of oxen. Mr. Mathis cut the bows in the yoke of these last two with an axe which released them, but the first two which fell in were dead when help came to them. They were drawn out with the aid of ropes.

I arrived safely at home on the third evening after leaving Alto. I spent a month at home, excepting a short time on a visit to relatives living in and near the town of Mansfield. These relatives were Uncle John Greening (Mother's brother) and his family. Also there were my mother's sister's children, Cousins Sam and Gus Guy and families, and their sisters Fannie and Lizzie

Pegues and families. Having been with them so much in earlier youth I had learned to love them, and desired to be with them a few days before I returned to Texas.

CHAPTER XII

NEW ASSOCIATIONS AND WAR CLOUDS

The first week in September, 1860, I was back in Rusk again. Some changes had been made in the school. Professor Mitchell had accepted an offer to take charge of the Masonic Institution at Henderson, and was to begin work there January 1, 1861. He taught the advanced class in Rusk until the end of the year. I had to give some of my pupils lessons in the country, and this made it necessary for me to keep my horse Sir Robin. The rides gave me exercise and recreation.

This year, 1860, was long to be remembered in American history. The Democrats in the National Convention were hopelessly divided in the choice of candidates for president. Stephen A. Douglas of Illinois was nominated, but this nomination was not unanimous and part of the delegates withdrew from the convention and met elsewhere and nominated John C. Breckinridge. This put two men before the people as candidates for the presidency as Democrats. The Whig party nominated in its convention a third man for the office whose name was Bell. There was not a very great difference in the platforms of the two parties. The Whigs favored more power to be invested in Congress and the president than the Democrats were willing to agree to. A third party was organized a little preceding this time, known as the Black Republican party. This party opposed states' rights and Negro slavery, but the main plank in their platform was to destroy the institution of slavery and to free the Negroes in the southern states. They met in convention and nominated Abraham Lincoln as their candidate for president. At the general election in November Lincoln was elected. This caused dissatisfaction in the southern states because of his often expressed opposition to Negro slavery. The southern people could not see clearly what could be done with the Negroes if given their freedom and thus far they had gotten along nicely with them. The discussions in Congress at Washington had already caused a spirit of dissatisfaction and after the result of the election the people were showing some interest in military affairs. They did not look upon Mr. Lincoln as a wise statesman, but they knew that he was very firm in his convictions and his platform was before the world, and notwithstanding any promise he might make on assuming the reins of government. They felt that to 'free the Negro' would be his chief aim as president.

General Joseph L. Hogg organized a company of young men and named this company "The Lone Star Defenders." I joined them and drilled some with them but did not neglect my music pupils, and during the autumn I also taught a class in vocal music. When the year was gone and Professor Mitchell was ready to move to Henderson, he insisted on my taking the music department in the Masonic Institution there. Professor J. C. Miszner, a good music teacher, who had been in Henderson for several years, was still there, and I hesitated to accept the position. However, I was assured that there would be plenty of work for both of us, so I decided it might be best to make the change. I had been at Rusk from September, 1859 to December 20th, 1860. My acquaintance was not confined to the town and I had many good friends out in the country around, as well as in town, and I had learned to look on the place as home, and really felt sad when the time came to leave. I went to my own dear home to spend the Christmas holidays with loved ones there. This was my last Christmas with some of them and the last time I was with brother Wade.

With the beginning of the new year, 1861, I left home en route for Henderson. Friends at Keachie thought it best and safest for me to have a passport to take with me on the journey. They said that incendiaries and trouble makers were at work in that part of Texas through which I was going. The citizens were arresting all travellers and were making them give an account of themselves, and that a little paper signed by the citizens of Keachie, showing who I was might be of some benefit to me. I thanked them for this manifest interest in my welfare and told them it made me love them more than ever. I took the passport but I did not think I would need it, as Texans were good judges of men and I didn't think they would take me for a mischief maker. Father and brother Rufus went with me as far as Keachie. They joined me in thanking those friends for that passport which manifested their concern for me.

I had no trouble on my way to Henderson, but I was told there that some men of bad character had been hanged and were buried in an old graveyard not far from the town. I afterwards saw the graves of those men. They had been trying to induce the Negroes to organize and kill as many white people as they could and burn the town. But the Negroes in those days had not manifested any desire to change their manner of living and were cheerful laborers on the farms. Some of them were good carpenters but the majority of them cultivated the fields.

I had a good class of piano pupils. Professor Miszner, instead of being jealous, was kind and always willing to render me assistance. In fact, he was getting tired of teaching and wanted a smaller class not connected with the Institute. There was an absence of enthusiasm in our school. The people seemed engrossed with national affairs, and the children heard more conversations about the disturbed condition in the United States. The little bugle sounds of the mail coach driver were eagerly listened for. There was a spirit of unrest. News, news, the people wanted news. It began to come. The people of the southern states were talking about seceding from the United States and forming a separate government. It was evident that they could no longer live in harmony with the agitators of abolition, and in the interests of peace and harmony, and in the exercise of their constitutional rights the government of the Confederate States of America was organized by several southern states. All the southern states loved the Union. Their people were proud of the United States flag as it "waved over the land of the free and the home of the brave." But the representatives of the southern states in both houses of Congress were a hopeless minority. The institution of slavery had been handed down to them. It was not of their creation, but they were using it for the mutual benefit, and prosperity of both sections, North and South. State sovereignty was their belief also, and they were cleaving to it. They knew that the newly elected president was opposed to both of these and hence the uneasiness and unrest among the southern people. It had found its way into Texas. Texans remembered how long they had to wait before their state was received into the Union when they applied for membership on account of these questions; and they discussed the problem of secession.

My duty was in the schoolroom and I took no part in state affairs, but I could feel that there was trouble not far ahead of us.

When Valentines Day came I received sweet little missives under the name of Valentine from the old Rusk town in Cherokee County, which reminded me that I had not gone out of the memory of some of my friends among the young ladies there. These little valentines brought both pleasure and sadness, because the ominous changes ahead of us all at the time would perhaps prevent me from seeing them for years, and maybe never again.

When at Rusk I had boarded with Professor Mitchell's family after the first month at the Thompson Hotel, and of course I expected to continue with them at Henderson, but they were expecting Miss Em Reagan, a cousin of Mrs. Mitchell, from the southern part of the county. It was agreed that she would stay with them and attend school at the Institute. Professor

Mitchell had made arrangements for me to board at the home of Dr. Marshall, a Presbyterian preacher who was pastor of the church of that denomination at Henderson. I could offer no objection as this, too, was a good family, but much of my leisure time was spent, and in fact I was very often a caller at the Mitchell home after Miss Reagan came. I was approaching my twentieth milepost, an age which Cupid loves to use his bow and arrow on an easy victim. Up to this time he had steered away from me and had not attempted any attack, but now he was using his best tactics and surest aim. No use attempting a denial, his arrow was too well aimed. Was she beautiful? Yes. More so than anyone I had ever seen (except of course my mother, as no one would displace her, but I was away from the maternal roof now). More fascinating, she was, in conversation, and more entertaining than anyone else. The charm of her voice made me forget that I was claiming too much of her attention in the Mitchell home. She was not one of my pupils. She said she had never had the opportunity to study music and now other studies claimed her time. Professor Mitchell and family called her 'Cousin Em' and I acquired the same habit. It seemed easier than to say Miss Reagan. The confession I had made to myself must not be made known to her now, though I believed she cared for me.

There was, as before stated, unrest and manifest dissatisfaction among the Texas people. They decided to cast their lot with the new government, The Confederate States of America. Delegates from South Carolina, Mississippi, Florida, Alabama, Georgia and

Louisiana met in convention in the city of Montgomery, Alabama on February 4th, 1861, and organized the new government in the interests of peace and harmony, and in the exercise of their constitutional rights. Their adopted constitution was similar to that of the United States, but it fixed the term of the president at six years and not eligible to a second term. It guarded carefully the doctrine of the sovereignty of each state. It forbade the slave trade or the importation of slaves from any foreign country other than the slave holding states and territories of the United States. It forbade bounties and 'trusts' of any kind and provided a tariff for revenue. Jefferson Davis, at that time a senator from Mississippi in the United States Senate, was elected president. Alexander Stephens was vice president. This choice of rulers and the constitution pleased our people and at once steps were taken to secede from the Union and join the new government. Mass meetings were held all over Texas and a date fixed for a state convention composed of delegates from all the counties.

The convention passed an ordinance of secession. Sam Houston was governor then and was present. He advised against it and told the delegates they were making a mistake. This secession ordinance had to be ratified by a vote of the people at an election. This brought on more speeches and more discussion. When the delegates from Rusk County returned to Henderson they were met, as they left the stage coach, by a large delegation in a torch light procession and were escorted to the courthouse yard. Mr. Kelly, one of the delegates, when called on for a speech, said, "My fellow citizens, this is the proudest moment of my life because I see by this manifestation that my vote in the convention for the secession of this grand state from the United States is approved by the people of my county." Judge Frazier, of Marshall, was present, and at the conclusion of Mr. Kelly's speech arose from his seat in the audience and said, "Fellow citizens, from one standpoint, this is for me one of the saddest moments of my life. This manifestation proves that the people of Texas are very much in earnest, but I regret that our people have thought best to sever their relations with the United States government. If we ratify the act of the state convention and vote Texas out of the Union, let us stay out and not join another government. This country will be deluged in blood. Americans, whether North or South, will fight when their country calls them. I believe that as soon as Abraham Lincoln is inaugurated president he will try to force by arms, the seceded states back into the Union."

I mention these two speeches to show the different views of Texas men at that date. The election followed, secession carried, and Texas joined the Confederate States government. In his message to the Confederate States Congress, President Davis said, "We declare solemnly in the face of all mankind that we desire peace at any sacrifice save that of honor. In independence we seek no conquest, no aggrandizement, no concessions of any kind from the states with which we have lately been confederated. All we ask is to be let alone; that those who never held power over us shall not now attempt our subjugation by arms."

My music class seemed to take more interest in their lessons after the election was over and business in the town appeared to be normal. I received a letter from my father in which he said it would be better for me to come home as soon as possible because the change in our government was a reality and the outlook was gloomy. I wrote to him that I did not think it really necessary to go before the school session was ended, as it would show bad faith to quit my class without some better cause, and I was getting along as well as I could wish at that time. Really, I was not anxious to leave Texas then. My acquaintance and association with the pupils attending the Masonic Institute from the southern part of Rusk County had much to do with this answer to my father's letter.

There were many pretty homes in Henderson, made so by the cultivation of artistic flower gardens, and the fragrances issuing from them, when fanned by the gentle zephyrs in the twilight of the April evenings, made us forget sometimes the darkening political sky and the distant mutterings and thunders of war clouds, so soon to engulf this beautiful southland. Cousin Em and I were sitting on the veranda at Professor Mitchell's home one evening and I held in my hand a lily, broken from a cluster of them in the yard. Presenting it to her I said, "Do you know anything so remarkable about this flower that it was selected to show how much grander it is arrayed than Solomon in all his glory?" "Yes," she said, "That is the one that does not toil nor spin. It is without odor and yet it has had all the attention necessary to make it grow and develop in form and feature, and now it is perfect. You must remember that the lesson to us by this illustration is that God provides for his own and in his own way, and that while there are other flowers more attractive, perhaps because of their fragrance, this lily is sufficient to illustrate the divine truth that man's efforts to display his own imagined importance in the world are overshadowed by the simplest flower of the valley in God's hands." I said, "I must agree that your construction of the lesson is truly correct." She said, "Thank you, but I see cousin John coming home from uptown walking faster than usual. He must have some news." Coming out on the gallery where we were he said, "Good evening young folks, the news at the post office is that General Beauregard has fired on Fort Sumter; old Abe will use that as a pretext to declare war." I said, "No, Professor, I think he will not declare war, because that would be admitting that we have a government. We have read his inaugural speech in which he claims that we have no right to secede from the United States government. We are at war now."

I bade my friends adieu for the evening and returned to my room to think over the situation and make a decision as to what I ought to do. The people in times past, both North and South, had stood 'shoulder to shoulder' in times of trouble, but there were those who had always looked upon slavery as wrong. They had now become fanatical, and wrote and preached much about it, without considering the condition of the Negro in the jungles of Africa as compared to his happy condition (of course there were exceptions) with his master in the cultivation of the fields of the southern states. Now the subject found its way into the Congress of the United States, where its opponents were overwhelmingly in the majority. No new state was allowed membership in the Union unless it came in without States' rights and without Negroes as slaves, both of which the Constitution recognized. The Missouri Compromise, the Squatter sovereignty question, the Dred Scott decision, all caused so much wrangling that the states which had seceded, saw no other solution than a peaceful withdrawal and final separation. Wm. H. Seward, the secretary of state, was an able man and stood firmly with Abraham Lincoln, as a leader in the newly organized Black Republican party. After the election of the latter to the presidency, Seward was his legal advisor. They were both evidently wrong in denying that the Constitution gave any right to the states to withdraw from the Union, but they were in power now and the people must bow to their assertions. They seemed to have forgotten what history had given to the world; that an attempt was made in the convention which framed the Constitution, to give to Congress power to use the military force of the general government to compel the obedience of a state, but which effort met with signal failure. The right of withdrawal was recognized when the Constitution was ratified by the people, and it said that Virginia, New York and Rhode Island clearly proclaimed it in their ratification of the Constitution. But the progress of the government was so rapid that sentiment changed as to the expediency of such a measure, and the Northern people desired that the states be subordinate to the national government. Their majority in Congress and the fear of a withdrawal by the Southern States, no doubt, gave strength to this opinion. No amendment of this nature had been made, and the South was in the exercise of Constitutional rights in their desire for harmony and peace when they framed the new government.

Fort Sumter was in the territory of the Confederate States government and rightfully belonged to the Confederacy. General Beauregard not only fired on the fort but continued a bombardment until Major Anderson, who was in command, surrendered. It was not Beauregard's desire to dishonor the United States flag, but on the contrary, he allowed it to be saluted after the surrender. A cannon burst in this salute and a Union soldier was killed and several wounded, but not by Confederate guns.

The southern states were not a unit. Union sentiment was very strong. If all the southern states had joined in the organization of the new government at Montgomery, Alabama, the war that followed might have been avoided. Temptation then, as always, is wrong. The president no doubt looked upon secession and nullification as one and the same, and a little group of states setting up a government of their own was sufficient to invite disaster. He did not consider them out of the Union, but in rebellion, and issued a call for 75,000 men to be added to the regular army for ninety days. This, he thought, would end all trouble easily. In his inaugural speech he said, "In your hands my dissatisfied countrymen, and not in mine, are the momentous issues of civil war; the government will not assail you. You can have no conflict without yourselves being the aggressors." Of course we felt after his call for 75,000 men for ninety days that he did not look upon what he had said in his inaugural address as binding. As I had told Professor Mitchell, we were already in war and must take the consequences. Those southern states which had not seceded were called on for their quota of the 75,000 men to be added to the Union army. This call aroused them and they cast their lot with the Confederate states; too late to prevent war. If every men in the South must be killed; if ash heaps must be made of every home in the seceded states, and blood must flow in torrents, the president could not be changed now. This was our outlook and we must resist invasion. Love of country, love of home, love of right and justice was strong in the hearts of our people. So were the convictions of the president of the United States, that all men are created free and equal; and that he would not allow the carnage and destruction of his fellow Americans, and misery and suffering, to prevent the realization of his views and wishes.

CHAPTER XIII

TROOPS CALLED – BECOMING A SOLDIER

In the month of May a company of infantry was organized in Henderson. This company was composed of a body of our leading citizens in the town and surrounding country; men of families as well as men without families. It seemed to me that I ought to join this company as it would not be very long before all our men would be needed in the army which had become a necessity in the Confederate States government. I did not think I ought to go home just to say good-bye. I was now separated from my parents, brothers and sisters, and they had learned to bear this separation. They knew I was acting my part in the duties of life and had accustomed themselves to bear the separation. To go now just to say good-bye or to bid them farewell before leaving on an errand like the one before me, perilous and uncertain and ignorant of its duration, would be wrong. So I concluded it would be better to write to Father and Mother that I had obeyed my country's call and was already a soldier, and that duty had prompted my decision. I told them that we must be cheerful, having faith that I would return to tell them of my varied experiences in the army.

Our company was ordered to go to Dallas in June to be mustered into service. But the call was for a company of cavalry and ours was infantry. This made necessary some changes in the membership roll because some of our men would not go in a cavalry company. But we enrolled 110 men for duty. Officers were elected. These were R.S. Cumby, Captain; M.D. Ector, First Lieutenant; Giles S. Boggess, Second Lieutenant; and Dock Durham, Third Lieutenant. Then there were the non-commissioned officers, sergeants and corporals. I did not want to be an officer because I thought I was too young to command men. Captain Cumby said he was glad I refused to be an officer because he needed me for his company bugler. Jim Armstrong, a private in the company, said he wanted the office of first fiddler and wanted me as second fiddler. I told him that I intended to take my violin, if I could find room for it in the baggage wagon, and he must do the same and we could have music in camps until we would have to throw the violins away.

When it was known that ours was to be a cavalry company, only a few days passed before a drove of horses from the prairies were in town for sale. Some of them were gentle, but the others were unbroken and had never had a saddle on them. I selected a beautiful young horse about 14-1/2 hands high, of cream color with black mane and tail; but he could only be caught with a lasso and a whole week passed before he could be made gentle enough for me to ride. He never did agree to wear shoes and the only way he could be shod was to throw him and tie all of his feet together. I afterwards found this very inconvenient because in the rocky counties of northern Arkansas and southern Missouri, when a horse lost a shoe he became lame, and could not travel until the shoe was replaced with a new one. All the members of the company who did not own horses soon secured them.

The next thing considered was a uniform. Black coats with vests to match, brown (Huntsville made) jeans pants, black hats and black boots made of calfskin tanned leather were the adopted uniforms. It looked well enough but was very hot to wear in the summer; however, we wore them when ready to start. Nothing was said about the color of the shirt or cravat. Mine at the start was white and the neckwear was a black silk string tie. This, of course, was soon a thing of the past. Our company started without guns or pistols. I had a knife made in a blacksmith shop with a blade about six inches long, which I carried in a scabbard in the leather belt I added to my uniform. I needed the knife in camps to use when cooking during the first year of the war.

The evening before we left Henderson, I donned my uniform and called to say good-bye to Cousin Em. She could not prevent the tears that came to her eyes when she saw the change in my apparel. She said, "It really looks like you are going to leave us." I answered that I felt that way too, but my country had called and I was obeying that little word, duty, which meant so much. I had asked Professor Mitchell to collect the tuition due me and arranged my store accounts and paid for my board at Dr. Marshall's. Then I bade them all good-bye. I said to her that I had already told the professor and family good-bye, but I believed I would just run away and not say good-bye to her; at any rate we must not let our last evening together be sad, and we would not say anything to each other about the little secret we were hiding. It had found its way unbidden and we could not prevent it. I felt now on the eve of separation that it was too late to say anything about my love. The evening passed as always when with her, pleasantly and rapidly, and when I extended my hand for a final good-bye, I told her that I would never forget her and that, should I not be slain in my first battle, I would write to her and tell of my experiences. She said that she hoped I would not wait so long before writing, as there would be so much I could tell her, even if I should not get in a battle.

CHAPTER XIV

OFF FOR THE WAR

On the morning of June 8, 1861, our company was making its first move. We were riding four abreast and somebody was shooting anvils in the town, thus honoring us with a salute as we passed the courthouse en route for Dallas. We waved our hats in response to the many waving handkerchiefs in the hands of ladies on galleries and balconies and yard gates and fences, as we passed through the residential part of the town. When we got out on the Tyler road I dismounted and climbed up on a high rail fence to take a last look at those who were still waving their handkerchiefs. At that distance I recognized some of those lady friends and threw my hat in the air as high as I could to let them know how much that cheering was appreciated. I thought, but was not sure, that Cousin Em was in that group. Years afterwards she told me I was mistaken because at that time she was in her room and was asking the protective care of our God around me, and that I might be shielded from the destroying missiles of the invaders of our beloved southland. A long hot ride over sandy and dusty roads was our first day's experience. Our first bivouac was near a creek from which we got water for both horse and soldier. Before leaving Henderson we had agreed as to who would be our messmates. Mine were A.C. Rorrison, John Whitesides, Ed Sturgis and Sam Marshall, a son of Rev. W.K. Marshall, at whose home I had been a boarder. Mr. Rorrison was the oldest man in the mess. He was a lawyer and had come to Henderson to practice law. He came from Ypsilanti, Michigan, his former home. He was a Christian and a splendid man.

As messmates we knew we would need a camp outfit because the camp was now our home. We procured a large frying pan, a skillet and lid, some tin cups, tin plates, a coffee pot, some cheap knives and forks and a tin water bucket. We put these utensils in a wooden box with a lid fastened with hinges. We also put in provisions to last a week. I had bought a pair of blankets which I rolled and tied to my saddle. These were to be my bedding, with my saddle for a pillow. After cooking, eating supper and caring for Frank — this was the name I had given my horse — we arranged our blankets for a night's rest and sleep. Mr. Rorrison was my companion and 'bedfellow.' But there was no rest nor sleep for me that night. I was not accustomed to that kind of a sleeping place and although very tired from the day's ride I did not sleep. So when morning came I was not refreshed. But I arose early to make preparations for another hot day's journey.

We passed through Smith, Van Zandt and Kaufmann counties and at the end of nearly a week's ride we camped at Hunnicutt's Spring, four miles southeast from Dallas. This was a pretty little town near the Trinity River. The square, in the center of which stood the courthouse, was shaded by pretty trees and was covered with green growing grass. An inviting place it was for loitering or loafing. We spent the days there but went out in the evening to our camp at Hunnicutt's

Spring. It was not a bold spring, but continued running water enough to form water holes in a little branch sufficient for our horses, and some of them were large enough to furnish water for a good bath but not large enough to swim in. The Third Texas Cavalry Regiment was organized at Dallas, consisting of ten companies of over 100 men each. Gen. Hogg's company, "The Lone Star Defenders," from Rusk, were a part of this regiment and were designated Company C. The General was not with them at the time. Frank Taylor was their new captain. Our Company was enlisted as Company B. Elkanah Greer was elected colonel of the regiment; Walter P. Lane, Lieutenant Colonel; George W. Chilton, Major and M.D. Ector, Adjutant. Our company was armed with shotguns and holster single barrel pistols. These pistols were a useless weight on our horses, swung on the horns of our saddles. After organizing and enrolling we had to wait for the arrival of these guns, which finally came from San Antonio.

We left Dallas in July, 1861. Our destination was Missouri to aid General Sterling Price with his state troops, whom Gen. Lyon of the Federal Army was pressing towards the southern part of the state. Our route was through the town of McKinney in Collin County and the town of Sherman in Grayson County, crossing the Red River into Chickasaw Nation, Indian Territory, and through Chickasaw into and through the Choctaw Nation to Fort Smith, Arkansas. We had Mexicans for wagon drivers. These wagons were drawn by mule teams. Old Mike, our company's wagon driver, knew very little about driving a team of any kind and in rough roads was sure to let the wagon get turned over, emptying its contents into the dirt, and sometimes making us go hungry by getting our provisions too full of dirt to use. He got across Red River without accident at a good ford, but after he was on the Territory side of the river there came a wall of water eight feet high, caused by heavy rains north of us, and overwhelmed a wagon and team about midway of the river. The mules were drowned and the wagon and contents were demolished but the driver, being a good swimmer, got out safely. A part of the regiment had crossed at this place but our company crossed where we had to swim our horses.

Frank swam like a deer, only his head above the water, and he carried me safely across. Of course, I got very wet. I noticed that some of the horses swam in such a manner that their riders kept their feet dry by lifting them up in the saddle. I saw two horses which could not, or would not, swim, and had to be pulled across the river with ropes, and one of them died after being pulled across.

The Indian Territory through which we passed was a beautiful country then. Some of it was heavily timbered with no undergrowth, and with grass high enough to easily hide a deer. There were some prairies and some little mountains and valleys. The Indians lived in little villages of huts for houses and there were some patches of corn and watermelons.

Some members of our regiment went to an Indian war dance one night while we were in the Choctaw Nation. They asked me to go with them but I told them that they could give an account of it the next day. I was tired and Frank was too and I wanted him to rest. They reported it to be a strange affair, but not interesting enough to reward them for their long ride.

On our last day's travel in the Indian Territory, we halted about noon and camped near a little river of clear still water that came from the Arkansas River, which was full to overflowing. After we had fed our horses and eaten lunch and were resting under the trees in the dense shade, this little river of clear still water tempted a plunge, and soon there were hundreds of men enjoying a swim. I joined them without saying anything to my messmates. The river was about 200 yards wide. I decided to swim across it, but I was not thinking about the danger. Being out of practice in swimming, I secured a piece of plank about eight feet long and ten inches wide which had floated out of the river and had lodged near our camp. I used it to push ahead of me for safety and to prevent my getting tired. On nearing the opposite bank, I saw the largest moccasin snake I had ever seen, coiled near the edge of the water. I steered around it and rested a little while on the bank. It was certainly a dangerous looking creature and I had nothing with which to kill it and so left it undisturbed. I had come across the river so easily I didn't think I would need my plank on my return swim, and started back without it. I was enjoying the swim until within about twenty feet of the bank, when a large wave from a log two men were playing with a few yards to my left, passed over my head and strangled me. I made strenuous efforts, but could not swim any farther and was sinking when I heard one of the men say, "Look yonder what we have done." They saw the wave strike me and they both swam to me. I caught at the body of one of them and scratched him a little, but he raised my head above the water and I caught my breath. At once all fear was gone and I asked them to get on each side of me and let me rest my hands on their shoulders. In this way we swam to the shore easily. I thanked them for saving my life. One of them said, "We caused the trouble and are not entitled to any thanks. Of course, it was unintentional, but if you had gone down we would have always felt that we drowned you." I told them I could not understand why I could not swim after being strangled. One of them said, "That was because you got scared, and you must never get frightened in the water, no matter what may happen." I told him that I had learned a good lesson and hoped I would always remember it.

I told my messmates that evening of my experience in the water. Mr. Rorrison said, "That accounts for the rumor that went through the regiment this evening that a man was drowned in this river here since we stopped. Nobody could tell his name nor his company. Your accident, no doubt, was misunderstood and a report of 'came near being drowned' grew to 'drowned.' We will have to look after you from now on; that would have been a fine report to make to Miss Em, that we had lost you in this Indian river. I feel very glad that you got out all right." I said, "I appreciate every word fully that you have said; false alarms as well as other reports grow in magnitude sometimes by repetition, and may result in harm." I always felt that I was very fortunate in having Mr. Rorrison for a messmate and companion, and the longer we were together, the stronger was the tie that bound us.

A private soldier in the army is like a wheel in a watch, a part only of its mechanism. His duty is to obey orders, but ours was a citizen soldiery taken from the various occupations of life. Of course, we were anxious to know what was planned for us as well as to know what was occurring in every part of the Confederate army. Off duty, both officers and privates were associates. Captain Cumby had asked my messmates to arrange our sleeping places near his own, because I was bugler and must sleep nearby, so that in case I did not wake up soon enough he could call me to sound reveille at daylight. Sometimes he would arouse the whole company before he succeeded in waking me. I slept soundly at night when not disturbed, and sometimes I failed to wake up before being called. His mistake was in not having me in his mess. Mr. Rorrison and I were often with our officers at night after suppertime and in this way we would learn of contemplated army movements. We had been frequent associates in Henderson with these officers and this was not left off in the army except when on duty. As a rule a private soldier is not in a position to know of expected army movements nor the strength of his own army nor that of the enemy. He gathers his information from results and by listening to those who are in a position to obtain information.

Mr. Rorrison and I kept pretty well posted. Ben McCulloch of Texas had been commissioned a brigadier general and been assigned to duty in the Western Department. Our regiment, the Third Texas Cavalry, then only known as Greer's Regiment, was to form a part of his brigade as soon as we arrived at Fort Smith, Arkansas. I had been supplied with a double barrel shotgun and a pair of holster pistols at Dallas, in addition to the brass bugle Captain Cumby had secured for me before we left Henderson. I was enrolled as chief musician there, and also at Dallas, and was exempt from guard duty at night. Otherwise I shared the duties of a private soldier. But I was not exempt from this duty after Colonel Greer appointed a regimental bugler at Dallas. Charley Watson got the appointment.

Col. Armstrong and I would take our violins out of the baggage wagon at night when favorable opportunity offered, and we would entertain the 'boys' with music. We were all boys in camp. We frequently played cotillions and reels for them to dance. They would form a 'full set' by tying a handkerchief around the left arm of those who were to act as ladies as partners. Often there would be a hundred or more men present to listen to the music, as well as to 'look on' at the dance. Some of our officers would take an active part in the dance.

When we arrived at Fort Smith we learned that we were badly needed at once in Missouri, where a Federal army was driving General Price southward. We made no stop at Fort Smith, but hurried on after fording the Arkansas River, and were soon on the road en route for Springfield, Missouri. When we passed through Fayetteville, Arkansas, we were greeted joyfully and received a royal welcome. Those people were getting news that Gen. Price had fallen back from Springfield and that the Federals were coming rapidly in the direction of Fayetteville. Of course, they were glad to see us, a thousand well mounted fine looking men from Texas, armed with shotguns and coming to defend them. How could they help being glad to see us! The ladies manifested the greater joy, waving their white handkerchiefs and clapping their hands. We could not help yelling, "Three cheers for Fayetteville," which was echoed by the entire regiment. I know those ladies felt safer when we had passed through the town and were between them and the Federal army. Our route now was through a broken country; hilly and rocky and the road very rough. Between Fayetteville and Cassville it crossed a creek many times. This creek was winding its way through that mountainous region towards the Arkansas River. The water was clear and swift and in some places the bed of the creek was the road.

After we got into Missouri, we camped a short while at a large spring which emptied its waters into a clear running creek. There were some large apple orchards in north Arkansas and south Missouri. The apple trees were heavily loaded with fruit. The apples were of good size but none of them ripe. We ate some of them without cooking, but they were much more palatable when stewed or baked and sugar added. The corn crops were good and we were supplied with roasting ears. These, added to our flapjacks and bacon, made a good menu. The flapjacks were made of flour and water well stirred with a spoon, a little salt added, and fried in a pan of hot grease. We made the flapjacks when we didn't have time to bake biscuits or cornbread. My messmates were all good cooks by this time. We had been out long enough to learn this skill. Sam Marshall was our best biscuit maker, an art his mother had taught him at home. John Whitesides was better at making cornbread. Mr. Rorrison, Ed Sturgis and I were about the same in frying a beefsteak and making coffee. Each had his evening to go after corn for the horses. The Quartermaster would buy a field of standing corn or a barn of ear corn and we would get what our horses needed. The man to go after it would make a bag of his blanket by tying the corners together and in this way could bring enough for the night.

When the hot days of August came, there was no time for resting. We had to reconnoiter to ascertain the position of the Federals, and sometimes make forced marches, and there was so much dust that sometimes it was difficult to recognize the face of a companion on these marches. Our company was out one day riding across a scope of wooded country. Matt Barton and I were riding together, when we found a well dressed man in Federal uniform lying on the ground with face upturned, stiff in death. He had been shot from his saddle in a skirmish and left to his fate by his comrades. Matt said, "Poor fellow." We did not search the body for anything, but left it untouched.

This was our first introduction to the sad results of war. The fresh shot holes in the trees around, showed that there had been a picket fight there, and this young man being left in the woods was sufficient evidence that his regiment or company had been forced to leave these woods hurriedly. We realized we would soon have to do some fighting. This day's marching through these woods was continued until after dark in the evening; when we were halted to rest for the night, it was without food or water for man or horse. I tied Frank, after taking off my saddle, and spread my blanket, I thought, on the ground. Making a pillow for my head with my saddle, I was soon asleep. I awoke the next morning to find the dried carcass of a hog about three feet from my face and many rocks under my blanket, but I had slept soundly until aroused by a bugle call to saddle up and mount. We were soon in line and on the march. We went about three miles to a spring where we were halted to prepare and eat breakfast.

General McCulloch's brigade was composed of Greer's Third Texas Cavalry, Col. Hebert's Third Louisiana Infantry and Churchill's Arkansas Cavalry. These regiments were full then, not having been in battle, so it looked like quite an addition to Gen. Price's forces. McCulloch's personal staff consisted of James McIntosh, Captain and acting Adjutant General; L.L. Lomax, First Lieutenant and Inspector General. Frank Armstrong was volunteer aide-de-camp, and Major Dillon, Commissary; Major Montgomery, Quartermaster; and John Henry Brown, Major and aide-de-camp. These men were prominent in the service later on.

CHAPTER XV

BATTLE OF WILSON'S CREEK

It was said that General Sterling Price had been an avowed Union man and had entered into an agreement with General W. S. Harney, the Federal commander in Missouri, to uphold the Federal government, but General Lyon was assigned to the command of Federal troops in Missouri, superseding General Harney. Price was said to be a Union man on patriotic principles, but Mr. Lincoln's plan of procedure made a complete change in his convictions. Compelling the abolition of slavery by force of arms, as mapped out by Mr. Lincoln, was something he could not endorse. So he called on Missourians to rally under the standard of the state in defense of its rightful government and the institutions of this section.

At the time I knew nothing of these things, but I knew that our brigade was in Missouri to help Price. General Lyon had gotten possession of the arms and munitions of the state, and at once made an invasion of that part of the state. Those Missourians who understood the real cause of Gen. Lyon's invasion, at once called for volunteers and raised companies and regiments, and went to Gen. Price under the state flag, to dispute the possession of their territory by Federal troops. It was certainly a test of patriotism for the Missourians. Armed with shotguns and squirrel rifles, with their powder horns and shotbags, they must dispute the invasion of their country by well armed, equipped, and disciplined Federal soldiers; and face them on the battlefield.

It was in this condition that Gen. McCulloch found them in the southern part of Missouri. He offered his brigade in support, but Gen. Price placed himself and his army under the command of Gen. McCulloch. We learned afterwards that the Missourians didn't like this. They knew Price but did not know McCulloch. Gen. Lyon, with 12,000 Federal soldiers, was at Springfield preparing for an advance south to attack Price, and this was not the time for disagreement. They were told, however, that being placed under command of General McCulloch was only for this emergency and was not permanent.

On the evening of August 9th we were ordered to move forward to Wilson's Creek, and after supper, to take up a line of march to Springfield to attack the Federals at daylight. A heavy rain fell on us and the order was countermanded while we were at the creek. We had supper but were not permitted to unsaddle our horses. We slept some, holding our bridle reins in our hands. We were awake at daylight the next morning, and ate a hastily prepared breakfast. I tied Frank to a little sapling and told Mr. Rorrison that I would go to the ford of the creek, some 200 yards distant, and wash my face and get some of the dust accumulated the day before out of my eyes. While at the creek I heard a cannon shoot nearly in front of me. A shell passed over and burst a little to the left of where Frank was tied. The shells were coming over and bursting fast by the

time I got to him. Our regiment was moving out on the
Springfield road by the time I had untied and mounted
Frank, but I soon overtook them. We were formed in
line in rear of some of Price's Missourians to give them
support when necessary.

A battle was on and the main force of Lyon's Army
was coming in our direction. We were in a dangerous
and most unpleasant position, sitting on our horses
listening to minnie balls whistling by us on their deadly
mission. There was no music in them, nor in the cannon
balls and shells passing over us from the batteries firing
at us over the coming Federals. Mr. Rorrison said, "See
that Missourian shooting and loading his rifle, he certainly works fast." "Yes," I said, "He is a man after my
own heart, I wish we could get around those fellows in
front of us and take that battery which is making us
dodge so much." Captain Chisholm of our regiment,
who was just in rear of his company near us, noticed the
dodging and said to his men, "Boys, you mustn't dodge"
and just as he said it, a cannon ball passed over him and
ducking his head he said, "Except when them big ones
come." The Federals commanded by Gen. Sigel were,
by this time, nearly in our rear with a battery and a body
of infantry. They had crossed the creek where I was
washing my face when I heard the first shell pass over.
But the Third Louisiana Infantry and Churchill's cavalry were looking after Sigel. The troops we had been
ordered to support were on the side of a hill just across
and north of the Springfield road. The Third Louisiana
Infantry not only drove Sigel back, but captured his
battery, and the Federals were on the run, that is, what

was left of them. General McCulloch was with the Third Louisiana Infantry when they took Sigel's battery on a rocky hill. After a time, our regiment was ordered to the right of our unpleasant position, and to charge the battery which had opened the battle on our right, but we were too late. The Third La. Infantry had not only taken the battery, but put the Federals to flight, 'every man for himself.' When Gen. Lyon's part of the army saw us coming it caused a panic among his troops. They got news that Lyon was killed and this added momentum to their flight across that cornfield and back towards Springfield. This battle lasted only about six hours, but it seemed a long time to me. There was no cessation of the roar of small arms and the thunder of artillery until the Federals were routed and fled.

This would have been an easy victory for Gen. Lyon's army if Gen. Sigel had made his attack without firing on us first with his cannon. We had no pickets in front of us. I never knew why, but somebody was to blame. If it had not rained on the evening of August 9th and stopped us we would have made a night's march and attacked the enemy at Springfield at daylight August 10th. That was the plan. Lyon had planned a daylight attack on us at Wilson's Creek and the rain did not stop him, but I don't know that it rained on his troops. Sigel's cannon gave us notice of his presence. We went to Springfield the next day but the Federals had not stopped there. They were on their way to St. Louis.

McCulloch was censured for not pursuing the fleeing enemy beyond Springfield. In my opinion, this censure was wrong. He was in the field and knew the situation best. We had too many camp followers called 'independent companies,' not subject to his command, who were not only a nuisance and 'eating out' the citizens where they marched and camped, but were very much in the way and could not be depended on in time of need. And Gen. Price had so many unarmed men who had rallied to his standard and had to be taken care of while waiting for guns. Those of his soldiers who fought so nobly at Wilson's Creek (or Oak Hills) needed rest. All of these things were to be considered, and in addition to these, there were Arkansas state troops at the battle of Oak Hills or Wilson's Creek who might be called at any time away from McCulloch's command. His decision not to follow Sigel proved to us that he was a safe commander and worthy of our confidence and support.

CHAPTER XVI

A WESTWARD MOVE
HARDSHIPS AND SICKNESS

We returned to the battlefield of Oak Hills or Wilson's Creek, leaving Gen. Price to look out for himself until he needed us again. The awful stench of the three or four days old battlefield forbade a stop there, so we continued our march westward until we arrived at a spring in southern Missouri which was a basin of clear bubbling water so large that a swift running little river started out from it. We were camped there for several weeks. My boots had worn out and as some of the company were having boots made at a shop a few miles away, I went to Captain Cumby and told him of my condition, and asked him to lend me five dollars to have a pair of boots made. My reason for the request was because I had enlisted in the army without money and he had promised that I should have it from him in case of necessity. And he had said that I would not need any money before we would be paid as soldiers. He declared that he was sorry but could not help me because he did not have any money. Matt Meyers, a merchant when in Henderson, and now a member of our company, did not wear boots. Matt had just had a pair of new shoes made because his old shoes were so badly run down and worn out on the side that he could not wear them any longer. Hearing what Captain Cumby said to me, Matt called me and said, "Cater, here are my old shoes; I give them to you till you get some new boots made." I said, "Matt, you wear number eleven shoes; I could not get the toes of your shoes in my saddle stirrups. Lend me five dollars to have some boots made and I will return your money when we draw our wages." Matt said, "I have the money, but you will get killed, and den I lose my money if I lend it to you." I was not in a humor to say any more to him, but the ground was so rough with rocks, that the same evening I hunted up old Matt and asked him to tell me where he had thrown his old shoes. I found them and had to wear them three weeks before I could have a pair of boots made. Luckily, we had to stay at that camp three weeks. Matt's shoes being too large for my stirrups, Frank got a good rest. A man from Henderson was coming to our regiment and gave us notice of his intended trip. He said he would bring letters from friends to our company and would carry all letters the boys would write to their friends back with him. When he came many of the 'boys' received letters from home. I received one from Cousin Em from her home in Rusk County. I had received no news from my home, so this letter was the nearest to home for me. I substituted my old fiddle box for a table and answered that letter. The following is a copy of the letter I wrote. It came into my possession, with others, after her death. She had taken care of all the letters I wrote to her when I was in the army.

> Regimental Encampment
> Clear Creek, Green County
> Monday, August 22nd, 1861

Miss M. Em Reagan
Iron Mountain, Rusk County, Texas

Dear Cousin Em,

A welcome communication from your gentle pen came to me at Fort Smith, Arkansas on July 28th. It came like a refreshing shower on a drooping plant, for up to that time I had heard nothing from home nor from you since I had left Henderson; and I was becoming despondent. On yesterday I had received another white winged messenger which I read and read again with pleasure. Until now I have not had an opportunity to write a letter to you. I am glad to learn that you enjoyed the remainder of the school term and that the examinations at the end of the session passed off with much credit to the young ladies of the Institute, as well as to its principal, Professor Mitchell. I would have been glad to have taken a part in hearing some of the classes and especially those in which you were a member.

You say that Sulphur Springs will be a place of fashionable resort this summer. I do not suppose that you will offer any objections. I would like to be one of its visitors, but you see how it is. I will just have to imagine that I am there, and that together we will watch the bubbling water as it gushes from that large basin and flows away, leaving the traces of iron which add to the real value of the cool water. Our camp here is about twenty miles northwest from Springfield, Missouri, and is near the largest spring I ever saw. It starts as a little river of clear running water which abounds with trout and other fish, but we cannot catch them because they see us as we approach, and then dart away. Though we tried hook and line and tempting bait, they cannot be enticed away from their safe retreat behind rocks which hide them from us. We are near some of the finest apple orchards in the world. The apples are not ripe yet but the trees are loaded with them and bend the branches on which they are suspended. Our 'mess' cooks some of them, and if we had some of that rich milk and delicious honey you mentioned in your letter, we would certainly enjoy both with our cooked apples. I am substituting my fiddle box bottom for a table to rest my paper on while I am writing.

Colonel Ector, our adjutant, is, I think, carrying out his promise to you in occasionally looking after the welfare of 'that little lost sheep.' He asks me to present his kindest regards to you. He is a brave soldier as well as a kind gentleman. I think lots of him too. I might venture to electioneer some, as requested, for you, as I sometimes see him looking at an ambrotype which he carries with him; but I fear I might be trespassing on sacred ground and more than that, 'hateful.' It seems to me that it would be safer for me to look after my own fences.'

You will remember that in my letter written at Dallas, I was not as well pleased with the prairies as I had expected to be, but at this time I had not seen the prettiest prairies of Texas. On our road from Dallas to Red River, we passed across prairies that were beautiful beyond description. The beauty and elegance of the prairies of Western and Northwestern Texas were more than I had expected to see and I must say, as did the Queen of Sheba on her visit to King Solomon, that "The half had not been told." But the prettiest country I have seen is in the Chickasaw Nation in the Indian Territory. I wish I could tell you of its beauties. The mountains, valleys and prairies of the Choctaw Nation are also beautiful; but who could wish to live there while its inhabitants are Indians! And yet they were kind to us while we were in their country.

No doubt you have by this time, heard of the battle of Oak Hills (Wilson's Creek). Well, we were there. I had an introduction to what is meant by war. Captain Cumby, the other officers and the entire company from Rusk County, acted their part well, and I believe that Rusk County must feel proud that these men represent that county in the Confederate Army. If I could be with you I could tell you much about the experiences of the day, but I am sure I cannot write them. We were expecting this battle and yet it commenced when we were not ready for it to begin. The Federals under command of General Lyon attacked us at daylight on August 10th. About 1 o'clock PM the noise of

battle ceased. Gen. Lyon had been killed and his army had
fled in utter defeat. Our victory was complete.
We will leave this place tomorrow and march southward.
It is the present intention to spend the winter near the line
between Missouri and Arkansas. But, of course, none of us
know what is in store for us. I am well. Should you get an
opportunity to send a letter, direct it to Fort Smith, Arkansas, in care of Captain Cumby, Greer's Regt., McCulloch's
Brigade. With my best wishes for your welfare and happiness and with kindest regards to those who inquire about
me I remain,   Respectfully, your friend Doug J. Cater.

From this camp we went to Pineville and then to
Carthage. Our regiment was at Carthage several
weeks. Our camp was near a spring at the base of a hill
or small mountain. The water, about four feet wide,
issued out of this mountain base, cold, swift and clear.
It was necessary for me to do some clothes washing at
this spring and the cold water made my hands ache
before I could get a garment washed. But with an
abundance of soap I managed to make my shirts feel
like they had been washed, although they didn't look
much like it.

The nights and mornings were quite cool, but much
of the day was warm. The apples in the nearby orchards
were ripening and this gave them a much better flavor.
Some of our men had contracted measles and were in
temporary hospitals in Carthage. I visited them and
found them getting well and not needing special assistance. Our regiment made a raid from Carthage into
the state of Kansas to ascertain conditions and to intercept a reported advance of Lane and Montgomery,

noted Jay Hawkers of the Federal army. Our trip was
unnecessary because news came to us that they had
returned to northern Missouri. When we returned to
Carthage we found orders awaiting us to go to the
assistance of Governor Jackson, who, in command of
state troops, was at Neosho, Missouri. General Price
had already come to his rescue when we arrived.

The legislature of Missouri was in session at Neosho,
and formally seceded from the United States Government. Our armies were near and Governor Jackson
cast his lot with us. This action brought General Price
and his army under the Confederate States government. Missouri, although divided in sentiment, was a
slave state, and a majority of the people favored a union
with the Southern confederacy. This was in October,
1861. However, the United States government claimed
the allegiance of Missouri, and had an army of 50,000
men under the command of General Fremont in the
eastern part of the state. It was said that he was then at
Springfield, and we had rumors of his advance in our
direction. Gen. McCulloch's little army had been increased by the addition of Stones's Seventh Texas
Cavalry, Whitfield's Texas Battalion of Cavalry, Captain Good's Texas Battery, Young's Regiment of Cavalry and Crump's Battalion, but the Arkansas State
troops went home after the battle of Oak Hills
(Wilson's Creek). With this army, and Gen. Price's
troops we set out to meet Fremont at Springfield. This
general, however, overestimated the size of our army
and returned to St. Louis.

Our regiment was sent to Springfield. We camped a

few miles south of the town, and at night Captain Mabry and an old Texas Ranger, Captain Johnson, now of our company, volunteered to go into Springfield without arms and ascertain the true situation. They returned after midnight. Mabry was wounded in the arm and Johnson had some shot holes in his hat. They had fallen into a trap set for them in a hotel and had narrowly escaped with their lives. There was still a company of Federals camped in the town but the main army was marching toward St. Louis. The next morning we started south toward Fayetteville, Arkansas.

Before night I was taken sick. I had a chill which was followed by a burning hot fever. I was so sick I had to get off my horse and lie down on the roadside. Lewis Kelly, a member of our company, was riding with me. He would not leave me alone and dismounted, saying I might need him. I became very thirsty and drank some water from my canteen, but instead of satisfying my thirst, it made me vomit. Kelly said I vomited more than a quart of blood. It looked more like a gallon to me. This relieved the sick stomach but made me feel very weak. Kelly turned very pale in the face and I believed he thought I would die there on the roadside. I told him not to feel uneasy about me and that I would soon be better. After the almost deathly sick spell passed off, although I had a burning fever, I felt like I could ride to camp. With Kelly's assistance I got on Frank and we followed the regiment, which had camped for the night, when we overtook it. I did not want any supper and slept some during the night, but the fever had not left me when morning came. As we

were about to start on our march, Captain Cumby came
to me and said, "You must not ride on horseback today.
You are in a hell of a fix and must get into one of the
wagons." Kelly had told him how sick I was on the
roadside the last evening. I felt weak and had high fever
but there was no house, nor anybody living near that
place, and I was compelled to stay with the regiment. I
had to have help when I undertook to get into the
wagon. Instead of going to Fayetteville we went west
in Missouri until night.

The regiment camped in a beautiful valley near a
farm house. Although having been hauled in a wagon
the whole day, I felt better that evening. Mr. Rorrison
said he would take care of Frank for me and that I must
try to stay in that house. It was occupied by good people.
The lady said her husband was in the army and not at
home, but she could not forbid a night's shelter to a sick
soldier. She gave me a good room in which there was
a comfortable bed. I did not need supper. The next
morning Mr. Rorrison brought Frank to me and said
the regiment had orders to move south, and if the Jay
Hawkers did not get me I would find the regiment
somewhere in Arkansas when I got well enough to
follow. My hostess' father came sometime during the
night. He took care of Frank while I was sick. I didn't
have any medicine and had to depend on nature to
restore my health. Of course I was careful and prudent
and 'mine hostess' watched after my diet.

This family had an abundant supply of provisions for
the coming winter. There was a cellar full of delicious
apples and there was meat, flour and cornmeal, which

had been secured before the armies destroyed the mills in the country. They had dried apples and peaches and our soldiers had left them corn and fodder in the barn. As soon as I was well enough to enjoy eating a good meal of well prepared food, this lady supplied tempting viands and I soon found that I was glad for mealtime to come. I was in this house a week, and was getting strong enough to ride. I paid my board for both myself and my horse and started to Arkansas to hunt my regiment. This lady did not want to accept anything for my staying there, but I told her she could not afford that, but must make the soldiers pay for everything she let them have. The war was just beginning and she would be asked often for something to eat for both men and horses, before that country was rid of soldiers.

I had a long lonesome ride before I got with my regiment, stopping at farmhouses at night on the route. The people offered no objection when I told them where I belonged and why I was not with my regiment. It was camped twelve miles east of Van Buren on the Arkansas River near the mouth of Big Frog Bayou. "The boys" were hard at work preparing winter quarters. I joined them and we worked faithfully on our new quarters so as to make them comfortable for cold weather. We cut logs, and built cabins with them and used rocks and mud to build our chimneys and fireplaces. A few days after we were located in our winter quarters a gentleman from Henderson came to us bringing letters to our company and a little package for me.

In this package was a pair of nicely made woolen

pants, two pairs of home knit woolen socks, a cap to put on my head at night and a little note in pencil which said, "You may need these, from your friend M. Em Reagan." I cannot tell how I felt on receiving these appreciated and much needed articles. I thought sometime, somewhere, I would tell her, but now a returned note of thanks was all that could be said.

We finished our winter cabins when an order came for five companies of our regiment to prepare to go to fight Indians. Our company was chosen as one of the five and Adjutant Ector was placed in command of us. Colonel Cooper, who had command of this department before General McCulloch came, had with him several Indian regiments of Choctaws, Cherokees and Chickasaws and Colonel Simms' Ninth Texas Cavalry. He had recently been defeated in a battle with old Creek Chief Opothleyohola who had an army of Creeks, Seminoles and Comanche Indians. I never knew why these Indians were divided and had taken sides, one with United States soldiers and the other with Confederate states soldiers. Col. Cooper asked Gen. McCulloch for help. Captain McIntosh of McCulloch's staff was sent with 1,200 men to Cooper's relief. Our company with four other companies of our regiment was numbered in that 1,200.

The weather was cold and winter had set in when we started. My new wool socks were now needed sure enough. I was not wearing Matt Meyers' old shoes now. I put on a pair of those wool socks under my boots when riding and the other pair over my ears, and they prevented my feet and ears from freezing. By the time we got to Fort Gibson, the weather had moderated some and was warmer. Squirrels seemed to be plentiful in the timbered low lands we passed through, and Bill Isham of our company, an old hunter and I, bought some powder and squirrel shot at Fort Gibson to change our 'bill of fare' if we found any more hunting territory. Early the next morning we left the company for a hunt. When the weather became warmer I put my wool socks in my saddle bags, to be used in the next blizzard which was just ahead of us. We learned from our commander how far the troops would probably go before night and the route also. Isham said we could kill some squirrels and get to camp by dark. He killed a large turkey gobbler and I killed some squirrels, but we had a hard ride before we found our company. My messmates and I had broiled squirrels for supper, but Bill Isham had to wait till the next morning before his turkey was ready. Lieutenant Boggess, one of his messmates, had bought some canned oysters at Fort Gibson. After the turkey was dressed those oysters were put inside of it and the turkey was swung over a fire of burning coals, and by the next morning it was thoroughly cooked. At breakfast he called me to come over and eat a piece of turkey. It seemed to me that I had never tasted turkey as good as this one. The next morning came with another change in the weather. The snow was beginning to fall and our ride was across a prairie with the wind howling from the north. I had to protect my ears and feet again with my wool socks. The splendid woman who had sent them to me was doubly remembered and had merited the increased admiration of this Confederate soldier.

We came at nightfall to a timbered swamp where the switch cane was three or four feet high. After caring for our horses, we cooked and ate supper. Mr. Rorrison and I cut some of this cane and bent down some of it and spread our blankets on it on top of the snow. We were tired and slept soundly, but the next morning we found the snow under us had melted and our blankets were in mud.

But there was not time for anything but breakfast and we were soon out on the prairie again for another day in the cold wind. In the evening we halted in a skirt of timber and placed our wagons in corral shape because we had been informed that the enemy had selected this place to attack us. Our command had passed to Cooper and Simms at Fort Gibson and they were to meet us with their forces at this place, coming a different route from the one we came, but they had not arrived.

I was appointed Corporal of the Guard for the night, and had to place and relieve sentinels every two hours. An alarm was given about midnight that the enemy had discovered us and were coming to attack us. This was a false alarm, but it had the effect, however, of making us more vigilant. It was true that they had seen us, but this made them prepare to give us battle the next day. I, of course, knew nothing about Indian warfare, but I knew that the guard under my charge that night was expected to keep a good lookout for any signs that indicated an attack, and I was to report promptly to Capt. McIntosh.

He had an Indian guide with him who piloted us the

next day to the position of the enemy. McIntosh did not wait for Cooper and Simms. He believed that the 1,200 men under his command would not need additional help. This proved true. It was Christmas day, 1861 when we came upon the enemy some ten or twelve miles from where we had spent the night. Their pickets fired a few shots at our advance column and retreated to their main army which occupied a very strong position, fortified by nature on a high hill, a real breast work of rocks and standing trees, and behind these they were waiting to receive our attack. We formed a line of battle in front of them. Bullets and arrows were coming pretty fast. A feathered arrow passed in front of my face just before we were ordered to dismount, and produced a strange sensation in me. After dismounting we were ordered to leave every fifth man to hold our horses. Henry Miller of our company was crying when the order came to charge because he had been detailed to hold horses. We made the charge in 'double quick' and climbed over the breast works. They fired volley after volley of rifles and arrows as we charged and climbed over those rocks. Seeing they could not stop us, they commenced running. We were then ordered to go back for our horses and get over those rocks with them as best we could and form in line and continue the charge. Some of those Indians were very brave and daring and would not leave, but continued to shoot. Of course, they were killed. One big feathered cap fellow stood out from the trees and continued shooting until he fell. I had shot both barrels of my gun and one of my holster pistols at him before he fell. I don't know who killed him. I thought I had, but some others of our company said they shot at that feathered cap Indian. We continued this running fire about seven miles and until there were no warriors in sight.

We captured all of their wagons, oxen, sheep, ponies, provisions, everything they had. Twenty-one Negroes and about three hundred women and children were taken, but only one warrior was captured and he was wounded. We lost fifty men as either killed or wounded, and we killed about two hundred Indians. Adjutant Ector, who commanded our five companies, said when trying to 'rally' them, "Men you fight well, but you scatter too badly." We camped on this battlefield when night came. This ended the Battle of Chustenahlah which is in the northern part of the Cherokee Nation, Indian Territory.

The next morning we were ordered to follow the Indians. I could not go with the company because Frank's back was so badly swollen from saddle bruises, I could not ride him, and I was detailed to remain with Lieutenant Durham who was mortally wounded the day before. A rifle ball had passed through his thigh and had shattered the bone. Poor man! He could not move without great pain and there was no hospital and no surgeon to help or give any relief. Awful neglect somewhere. Such an errand without a surgeon or medical supplies! I could only give him water and make him as comfortable as possible while waiting for the return of the company. They came back late in the evening and reported that they followed the trail of the Indians fifteen miles but did not overtake them.

On the day of the battle (Christmas) Henry Miller had taken a Negro boy up behind him on his horse late in the evening and was passing a group of Indian women when one of them claimed him as her child. Henry said when he put the little boy on his horse, "I've captured me a Negro," but he had to give him up. The woman could not talk English, but her signs convinced our commander that the boy was her child and he told Miller to let her have him.

On the 28th we commenced our march back to Arkansas. I caught an Indian pony and rode it, leading Frank. We met Col. Cooper who expressed dissatisfaction because McIntosh did not wait for his arrival before attacking the Indians, but as before stated, McIntosh did not think he needed Cooper. I really do not think he had any faith in Cooper or Simms after their defeat by old Opothleyohola. We learned from one of our captured Negroes that the old chief said when leaving his strong position, "No Cooper this time." The Indian women and children (squaws and papooses) and all the fruits of our victory were turned over to Cooper, except the pony I was riding and the twenty-one Negroes. We carried the Negroes to Fort Smith. Lieutenant Durham was hauled in a wagon as far as he could bear it. His sufferings were very great, and were becoming worse, so we left him and two men of our company to nurse him at the residence of Colonel Drew in the Cherokee Nation. Drew was a half breed Choctaw Indian and a fine man with a nice family. Durham died in a few days, not from lack of kind attention, but because there was no surgeon to relieve his suffering by amputating his bone shattered thigh.

We arrived at our winter quarters after being absent three weeks. When we passed through Van Buren on our return we were halted and formed into line, and a bucket of whiskey with a tin cup to drink out of was passed down the line for every man to take a dip or drink out of that bucket. This was intended for a 'treat' but I felt it was wrong. We did not need the whiskey and some of the men were made very drunk and boisterous, but there were no quarrels or fights. Winter quarters were twelve miles down the river from Van Buren and it was midnight when we arrived there.

A rainy wet spell of weather came on us and the streets of our camp were so muddy and soft that we had to make walks of sand to go from one house to another. Frank's back was still too sore to admit a saddle on him and my Indian pony was not suitable for a cavalry horse and it became necessary for me to buy another horse. A soldier of another company of the regiment had died and the captain of his company sold his horse to me. He did not suit me as well as Frank. He was a very fine horse but was hard to manage when excited and sometimes he would run away with me.

There was one strange thing about the horse. He could not see well at night and I had to guide him as a blind horse when I had any riding to do at night. Once Adjutant Ector asked me to go with him to Van Buren and call on some young ladies who were the possessors of a fine piano. He insisted on my going with him because he wanted company and because I could play the piano. He said we would hear some good music and we did, and the evening passed pleasantly, but the long twelve mile ride to the winter quarters over a rough road, and I having to pick out a route for my horse, overbalanced the pleasure of the evening's entertainment.

Another time I went with Captain Barker and Lieutenant Frank Daniels of Company C to an entertainment at night, ten miles distant from the winter quarters. Perhaps I did wrong because it proved to be a dance, but it was a change from the monotony of camp life. One place in the road was dangerous even in daytime and on both going and returning I had to dismount and lead my horse while the others passed the place, it seemed, without having to pay any attention to the road. My experience at the dance, however, prevented me from attending any more entertainments that winter. A soldier of our regiment, but a stranger to me, had been making calls at this home and was very much smitten with one of its occupants. For this he was not to be blamed because she was not only very pretty but good company. Unfortunately he was under the influence of too much whiskey on this occasion and did not want anybody besides himself to talk or dance with this young lady. During the intervals of the 'sets' of cotillions and reels some of the 'boys' present asked me to play some pieces on the fiddle. I noticed that this young lady liked my music and I was talking to her when the fiddler called out "Partners for a cotillion" and came for his fiddle. We agreed to be partners and had taken our places on the floor when her admirer came up in front of us and slipping his pistol belt so as to show a huge six-shooter objected to my dancing with 'his partner' as he called her. I really was sorry for him because I felt like I would be forced to use my cook knife on him if he attempted to draw his pistol. I said "You are altogether mistaken, this time" and placed my hand on the handle of my cook knife. Some ladies saw this motion and instead of screaming and running away, rushed between us, and paying no attention to me, took charge of the man. They led him out of the room and on up the stairs and told him to stay there and he stayed. There was no more interruption. I never saw that man any more. After this 'set' had ended and the young folks were seated, Captain Barker and Lieutenant Daniels came to me and said, "Cater, we are here to shed our last drop of blood for you if necessary, we saw everything that passed and are proud of you." I told them that I could not express how I felt towards them, but must confess it was good to know that I was not alone.

Some of the ladies came up to us and said that their guest would make no more trouble nor interruption to our pleasure, and that he would be ashamed of his conduct as soon as he was sober; and that we must not let this evening's occurrence prevent us from calling to see them again. They said that they had given this entertainment for the pleasure of some of our regiment as well as their own, and that they had enjoyed it and hoped that we too had enjoyed it and had a pleasant evening. I assured them that I had been royally entertained, and thanked them for their splendid generalship in managing a drunken guest who tried to interfere in their pleasant pastimes.

A little later on when the swamp in the river bottom was dry, the days sunshiny and the nights cool, I was tempted to take a hunt for ducks or whatever game might come in sight. I had some of the shot and powder left which I had bought at Fort Gibson on the Indian raid. I could not find Bill Isham, my old hunting partner, as he was out somewhere, so I ventured alone in the swamp on a hunt. I walked through the dense switch cane until I came to a log cabin on a hill, from where I could see the river. I had seen a swamp rabbit but I did not want it. I ventured up to this cabin to ask the people who lived in it if they could tell me how to find a road which would lead me back to camp. I was tired and wanted to go back without having to go through the cane. This cabin certainly looked lonesome in this dense swamp. There was a man in the cabin, and he said to me, "Do you belong to them Texans in winter quarters down on Big Frog Bayou?" I told him yes. He said, "Well sir, it is sundown and you can't go back there this evening. It is five miles down there and you have a long walk before you, did you come through the swamp?" I told him yes. He asked me, "Didn't you see any turkeys?" I replied, "No Sir." He then said, "Well, there is a fine drove of them in there somewhere, and there are some big bears in there too, but I expect they are like you Texans, still in winter quarters, but in a hollow log." I told him I had climbed over a big log and because the vines and canes were so thick at each end of it, I didn't look to see if it was hollow. He said, "Well sir, I know where that log is; it is hollow and I think there is a bear in it for the winter. A bear stayed in it last winter, and I am making up a crowd to hunt for him. Come in and stay with us tonight, we have plenty to eat." I thanked him and told him I would be glad to stay, but that he must give me an early start the next morning. He said, "I'll put you in a trail that leads out to the Van Buren road, and you may kill some game before you get to it." I spent the night with him and he gave me an account of some of his bear and turkey hunts. He had a dressed opossum on the roof of his cabin. He said he put it up there to take the frost. The night was cold but I slept warm in a good bed. His family was small. He had a wife and two children.

The next morning I went to camp without stopping to do any hunting. It was well that I hurried back because Mr. Rorrison by this time was uneasy about me, fearing I had lost my way in the swamp and had to stay out till morning.

Orders had come to get ready to break our winter quarters and march. We were to leave Big Frog Bayou and our log cabins for scenes of carnage and hardships just ahead of us.

CHAPTER XVII

ELK HORN BATTLE (PEA RIDGE)

General Price and his army went into winter quarters at Springfield, Missouri, but the Federal army under command of Generals Curtis and Sigel forced him to leave that place about the middle of February, 1862. Some of General McCulloch's brigade were at Fayetteville, and Gen. Price retreated to that place. The citizens on hearing that Price was retreating before the Federals, of course, were terror stricken, and as many as could leave went south, taking as much of their property with them as they could. The Third Louisiana Infantry and McRea's and McNair's regiments of McCulloch's brigade went north and passed Cross Hollows to support Gen. Price.

The Federals made an attack but were repulsed. This part of our army then returned to Cross Hollows. Gen. McCulloch came to them here, from a trip to Virginia. Young's, Mitchell's and Rector's cavalry also arrived. The Federal cavalry made a movement to the left of the army and took possession of Bentonville, Arkansas where Rector's regiment had been camped. Price's and McCulloch's armies retired to Fayetteville, finding the town deserted. The soldiers took possession of the bacon, pork, hams, shoulders and other provisions which had been left by the fleeing citizens.

Our regiment, after a forced March from winter quarters, got to the main army at this place. General

Van Dorn, who had been assigned to the command of
the Army of the West over McCulloch, arrived here
also, and assumed command. The weather was cold and
the ground frozen, and our infantry soldiers, just out of
winter quarters and making forced marches, were foot
sore, and many of them had to drop out of ranks with
feet too sore to march. Our regiment passed many of
them, and just now they were badly needed. The
Federals were farther south than they had ever been.
Sigel's command was at Bentonville, and Curtis' army
was at Pea Ridge near Elkhorn Tavern. They had been
informed that Van Dorn's army was coming to meet
them.

Captain McIntosh, hero of Chustenahlah, had
received a brigadier general's commission, and was in
command of a brigade of cavalry. Our regiment was
assigned to his command. His other regiments were
Stone's, Simms' and Young's Texas regiments and
Embry's Arkansas cavalry. General Albert Pike with a
brigade of Indian cavalry was also near us, but was
worth nothing to our army. The first cannonball that fell
among them, made them get out of reach of all further
danger. Our infantry needed some rest to get their feet
in better condition. Of course, I was not in a position to
know Van Dorn's plan of action, but anybody could see
that there was too great a hurry to bring on a battle
without a better preparation. When our brigade arrived
at Bentonville about 12 o'clock expecting to attack the
Federals there, they had left the town and were retreating towards Pea Ridge. Our regiment was ordered to
make a circuit to their left and cut off their retreat.

Lieutenant Col. Walter P. Lane commanded us on this day. We had left Col. Greer at Big Frog Bayou, but he came to us at night after our experience of this day. We made a hurried march but did not get to the place designated, in time to intercept the Federals. They were already there and in ambush. Two picket guards came galloping up to the front of our regiment calling out "Halt, surrender" and without waiting for a reply or response of any kind fired on us. We were riding in fours and this was our company's day to be at the head of the column. They were both killed, but their first shot killed my old hunting companion Bill Isham, who was in the next four just in rear of me. He fell from his horse and never spoke. A little farther back Sam Honey, another man of our company, was killed instantly. Lieut. Col. Lane was riding at the head of the regiment. Instead of forming us in line of battle, he wheeled his horse to the right and gave the command to charge. We made the charge as best we could both in front and to the right. We were met by a charge of Federal cavalry, but they were easily repulsed. They must have been trying to draw us into an ambuscade of infantry, and their cannons were fired on us fast and disclosed their position.

There was no further advance except in my own case. My horse became unmanageable under the bursting of shells from the Federal artillery. I saw my company wheeling and disappearing behind the decline of a hill, but I could not follow suit. My horse's head was toward the enemy and I could neither stop him or turn him. I was out in the main road. Two well mounted Federals were coming toward me firing their pistols. They came in gunshot of me and seeing I did not shoot, misunderstood my situation and wheeled their horses to join their comrades who were then on the run. Although my horse was at full speed I took a shot at each of those two men. Neither fell, but I had not missed them. They were holding to their horses' manes when they disappeared over the hill. They did not know that my horse was running away with me. After I shot at those two Federals, my horse seemed to come to himself and I got him turned toward a clump of trees and stopped him. I reloaded my gun without dismounting, by resting my gun on my left foot in the stirrup of my saddle. When I had loaded and recapped my gun, I was ready to go in the direction my company had taken.

Taylor Brown, whose horse had thrown him and run off, was the only man in sight. He said, "Let me get up behind you and we will get away from here." I said, "Taylor, where is the company?" He said, "Running like hell and we will be captured if we stay here any longer, don't you hear them damn Yankees coming?" I answered, "They thought we had orders to bag Sigel here." (Sigel was in command of this brigade of Federals.) Taylor answered, "Bag Hell, let me get up behind you." I said, "All right, Taylor, don't throw away your gun." He answered, "Damn the gun, let's leave here." I said, "Put your gun under that log and you get up on the log, and I'll ride close to it so you can get behind me." He did so but the horse threw him off. He tried again and the horse did some high jumping, but he could not throw him off. After a four mile fast ride we overtook some men of the company. In order to rest my horse Taylor rode behind a man on another horse, and about nighttime the regiment stopped to camp. Captain Cumby said, "Fall in men, call the roll Sergeant, I want to know how many men we have left." Only two men failed to answer to roll call. They were Bill Isham and Sam Honey. The Captain said, "I don't understand why we didn't get more men killed, we will never be in a worse place than we were this evening." The Federals were on higher ground and shot over us, I think, was the real cause of our not losing more men. We fed our horses, cooked and ate supper, which was our last meal until Saturday night. This was Thursday, March 6th, 1862.

Friday morning we had to saddle our horses and start without breakfast. Taylor Brown's horse had followed the company and was at our camp when we stopped for the night. We passed our battle ground very early, and I went with Taylor to the log where he had left his gun, which was found as he had left it. Sigel and his army had moved on as soon as we left them, and were in position and ready for action Friday morning. General Van Dorn went with General Price and his troops around to the left and attacked General Curtis's troops from the northwest. Generals McCulloch and McIntosh met the attack from the southwest. As our brigade came on the field, the battle was opened by a Federal battery about 400 yards on the right of our front. Gen. McCulloch was passing our regiment when the first shell exploded near us. He ordered Gen. McIntosh to take that battery; and gave orders for our regiment to stay in line and support the battery which was with him, and which had unlimbered and was ready for action. Gen. McIntosh charged with I don't know whose regiment, and took the Federal battery with a slight loss. Col. Greer had arrived and was with us then.

McCulloch moved forward with the battery which was with him and ordered Col. Greer to dismount and form in line just behind Pea Ridge. The General was dressed in a black velvet suit and wore a brown hat. He always carried a small rifle instead of a sword. He formed the Third Louisiana Infantry, Mitchell's, McRea's and McNair's regiments into line of battle. Gen. McIntosh was forming Embry's, Churchill's and Rector's regiments and Whitfield's battalion a little distance from Gen. McCulloch, when skirmishing commenced in front of this last line. McCulloch rode forward to reconnoiter the enemy's position, telling his staff to remain where they were because their gray horses would attract and draw the fire of the sharpshooters. He had not gone far into the brush when a company of Federal skirmishers saw him and fired.

Gen. McIntosh galloped down the line and meeting Captain Armstrong, said "I fear the General is killed; a whole company of skirmishers fired on him. He clasped the pommel of his saddle and fell forward, his horse plunging violently." McIntosh immediately ordered a charge by the whole line. It seemed that he could not stay in rear of the line to direct the battle, but waving his sword, was leading the charge when he was shot from his horse and was killed instantly.

The enemy was forced back and Gen. Pike's Indian cavalry came upon the field to scalp and plunder, but a shell from a cannon burst among them, so they disappeared and General Pike with them. He was next in command but could not be found and this part of Van Dorn's army was for the time without a commander. Colonel Hebert of the Third Louisiana Infantry was captured. He was the senior colonel of the brigade. The next in rank was our Colonel E. Greer and the command fell to him, but at that time he was holding the position which had been ordered by Gen. McCulloch and was in total ignorance of the deaths of McCulloch and McIntosh and the capture of Col. Hebert. I will give his report later.

Of course there was confusion. The Third Louisiana Infantry, not knowing that our regiment was dismounted and waiting for orders to move forward, mistook us for Federals and were coming towards us with "that yell," which seemed always to carry victory, and we, thinking we were attacked by Federals, were holding our fire for them to come nearer, (the underbrush was dense) when they saw our flag. They had not commenced firing. The sight of that flag brought joy to them and to us. There went up a shout greater than that of victory, from both regiments. Terrible would have been the slaughter if there had been a gun fired before the mistake was discovered. There was not a better nor a braver regiment in the entire Confederate army than the Third Louisiana Regiment of Infantry; and our regiment had merited a good name.

Our regiment was then ordered to return to where our horses had been left. Up to this time we did not know that McCulloch and McIntosh had been killed, but we knew that something was wrong because we were idle too long. Col. Greer ordered us to mount and we were in the saddle the balance of the day and night, frequently changing our positions. Saturday morning the enemy opened a heavy fire of artillery but there was no action on our part towards renewing the battle. Our regiment had not fired a gun and did not know why we were not ordered forward. I could not understand this. There was no further action of McCulloch's army. Some of the command, like us, had not been used except to change positions. About 10 o'clock on Saturday, we found that we were in the rear of our army to protect a retreat. Now read Col. Greer's report. I got in possession of this report afterwards, and am placing it here to show why the Federals have the reason to claim the battle of Pea Ridge among their victories.

"After consultation with my officers and finding it impossible to receive any orders from either McCulloch or McIntosh, I moved my regiment back to their horses and took a position in the field near where we were in the morning when the masked battery of the enemy opened up on us. I then went in person in search of Generals McCulloch and McIntosh. I soon met with the staff of the two generals who informed me that each one of them was dead and that I was the senior officer of the field. I made inquiry for General Pike and was informed he was not present. The firing had ceased on both sides before this. I at once assumed command of our remaining forces on the field. At 10:00 P.M. I determined to issue an order to take up the line of march at 1:00 A.M. and join Gen. Price. Dispatching a messenger with a statement of our condition, the number of our forces, accompanied by a copy of the order of march to the General commanding, giving time to return before 1:00 A.M. in case it did not meet his approbation. The messenger returned before the above stated hour with an order to move as soon and as rapidly as possible, and take a position on the telegraph road. At 1:30 A.M. we took up the line of march and before day, reached the telegraph road and there awaited further orders. About sunrise a message reached me from the commander-in-chief stating that the enemy was advancing. A guide was sent to conduct me to a position on the left of our army. When I reached a point not exceeding a mile from the right wing of our army, the fight was renewed by heavy cannonading on both sides. Very soon I reached my position on the left, forming the infantry regiments in two parallel lines and the cavalry in the same way with the head of these columns resting on the right of the infantry. I was instructed to hold this position and await further orders. After remaining in this position about two hours I received an order from Gen. Van Dorn to fall back on the Huntsville road, leaving one regiment to cover our rear."

It was now evident that Gen. Van Dorn had given up the fight. This seemed to our army very wrong. We had lost McCulloch and McIntosh, but many of our troops had not fired a gun and we were ready to make a forward move under command of Col. Greer, with every hope of success. Gen. Van Dorn certainly did not understand the true situation and was managing his troops, after hearing of the death of our two generals, to prevent any more losses. The Federals had been driven back and Gen. Price's forces had slept on their arms a mile from where the Federals had made their last stand. When the heavy cannonading, which Col. Greer speaks of in his report, had commenced on Saturday morning, I was expecting that we would be ordered forward in line. Col. Hebert of the Third Louisiana Infantry, who was captured on Friday morning, told his regiment, after he had been exchanged and was with them again, that the Saturday morning attack by the Federals was a feint to cover their retreat. He said that Gen. Curtis was in favor of surrendering his army to stop further carnage, but Gen. Sigel insisted on making the feint and retreating, and in so doing, he discovered that Van Dorn was retreating.

The Federals made no effort to follow us but they claimed a great victory and claimed that they had not only run us out of Arkansas but "clear on to Memphis, Tennessee." Our regiment had been left to "cover the retreat."

The infantry were passing us in the main road when a message came to Col. Greer asking for a man with the fastest horse in the regiment to take a message to Gen. Van Dorn, and I was sent with it. It was a folded paper and had not been opened. I made a hard ride through the brush on the outside of the road. I could not pass the infantry soldiers in the road and so had to take to the brush. When I overtook the general's staff I asked for Gen. Van Dorn saying I had a paper for him. Col. Dabney Maury said, "I am his adjutant, give it to me." I handed the paper to him. After unfolding it, he read it and gave it back to me saying, "Tell him to keep it." My ride had been fast and rough, thinking I was taking news of importance to the commander which might stop our retreat. Although only a private soldier I thought this retreat was wrong. I noticed that Maury smiled when he read the paper. Here is what it said, "General, I have captured three barrels of whiskey: What shall I do with it?" I tore up the paper and threw it away. I didn't take any message back. I was not only mad but badly (I don't know a more fitting word) whipped. I stopped on the roadside and waited till my regiment came up. I told Captain Cumby what Col. Maury said. The 'boys' had a good laugh at my expense. I never heard what was done with the three barrels of whiskey.

Late in the afternoon we were passing a little farmhouse near the road and I saw some soldiers coming out of the house with apples in their hands. I dismounted and went with others into the little house. There had been a barrel of small, red apples in the house but there only two left. Of course I got them. There had also been a pot of half cooked beans but these had disappeared except about a half a saucer of them. I ate these and one of the little apples but I gave the other one to Ben Turner with whom I was riding. Ben said, "That little apple did me lots of good." I felt stronger after eating the apple and beans. At night our commissary issued some cornmeal and bacon. I washed the dirt off a smooth rock which was large enough and flat enough to bake bread on. I put it on some coals of fire to get hot while I mixed some cornmeal and water in a large tin cup, making a dough which I baked on the rock. While it was cooking I broiled some slices of bacon on a stick over the fire and let the grease from it drop on my bread. I never enjoyed a supper as well as I did this one. This was Saturday night and our last meal had been on Thursday night and I was hungry. Pretty soon afterwards I was asleep on my blanket on the ground and rocks. If I dreamed I don't remember it, and I was not disturbed.

About sunrise Sunday morning Mr. Rorrison said, "Hey, man, you are the hardest man to wake I ever saw. I've been pulling at you for some time. We've got to leave here, so come eat some breakfast and saddle up." I thanked him for cooking breakfast for me. "Well," he said, "I had to, I couldn't get you awake."

That evening we camped in a brushy, broken, rocky region near a wild pigeon roost. I wanted to go to it. I had left my shot and powder in my saddle bags in the company wagon when we left winter quarters and didn't know where the wagon was. So I spoiled a half dozen buck and ball cartridges, saved the powder, and cut the shot and balls into little slugs to use for small shot. The roost was about two miles from camp. I asked a citizen who lived near where we camped to pilot me to the roost. He complied with my request willingly and we were soon at the roost. Pigeons are very noisy where they roost and when their numbers are very great they make a roar like distant thunder when they fly. This night was showery and cold. The moon was about full and the night was not very dark. I could see the pigeons in the trees and when I shot at them they would fly, but only make a circuit and come to the same place and settle in the trees again. I did not get many of them, but enough for several fries for our mess. It was after midnight when I got back to camp but I got a few hours sleep. We were now on our way back to winter quarters, but not to stay.

Sam Marshall suggested to me the next morning that he and I could go by a distillery in the little mountains not far off of our route and get a canteen of apple brandy. I agreed to this, feeling that it would be of some benefit to us in our continued exposure to bad weather. We had guessed about where the regiment would camp at night. We succeeded in our errand and were with the regiment before dark.

This was my evening to go after corn for the horses of our mess. I had to go to a field and pull the corn from the stalk. I don't know why this corn had been left ungathered in the field. I had been tasting the brandy occasionally during the cold ride of the day and by the time I got my corn pulled and into the sack, made of my blanket, the brandy had found its way into my legs and I could not put the sack of corn on my horse. The brandy had not affected my head but had considerably impaired my navigation. The men who had come with me after corn had paid no attention to me but had gotten their corn and left for the camp.

My horse seemed to take in the situation, and although usually quick and spirited, waited patiently while I made repeated attempts and failures to put the sack of corn across the saddle. When about to give it up and go to camp without my corn, I saw a stump by the side of the rail fence near where I had come into the field. I dragged the corn to that stump and went back after my horse who was still waiting and watching me. Leading him up close to the fence I succeeded in getting the sack of corn on the stump. With one foot on a rail in the fence and the other on the stump I pulled the sack to the top of the fence, and then putting both feet on the stump, the horse standing very still, I pulled it across my saddle and climbed on behind the saddle, and in this manner went back to camp. Mr. Rorrison, always a friend in time of need, took charge of the corn. Placing my left foot in the stirrup I dismounted, but my legs had not sobered any. The 'boys' enjoyed the situation but were ready to give any necessary assistance.

Troubles seldom come singly. After I had fed my horse, a sergeant came up to me and said, "You are detailed Corporal of the Guard tonight." I told him I could not obey orders this time. He went off laughing. I don't know what he reported but I heard no more about it.

The next day we continued our march to Little Rock and waited there for our wagons which we had left at winter quarters. When they came I was minus saddlebags, violin and clothing too, except what I was wearing. Old Mike, our wagon driver for the company, had let the wagon get turned over at a bad place in the road. My violin and case were mashed into too many pieces to pick up, and old Mike, instead of putting my saddlebags back into the wagon, had left them on the ground where the wagon turned over.

Rain set in and we had a spell of wet weather. Only

those who have had experience in camping out with no shelter can know what wet weather brings to the campers. "Disagreeable" hardly supplies the word. It was "bad."

CHAPTER XVIII

WE CROSS THE MISSISSIPPI
I FIND BROTHER RUFUS

We continued our march to Duvall's Bluff on White River. The Western Army was transferred to the Army of the Tennessee which was at Corinth, Mississippi, under the command of Generals Beauregard and Bragg; Beauregard commanding the department. Our regiment was dismounted at Duvall's Bluff and we went on board a steamboat to go to Memphis, Tennessee. Our horses were sent back to Texas. This was the last time I ever saw my horse which had proven to be a faithful animal, and I felt like I had parted from a very dear friend. We went down White River to where it empties into the Arkansas River, then down that river to the Mississippi River, and then up that river to Memphis, Tennessee.

I was sick when we arrived at Memphis and it was with great difficulty that I marched out two miles to a camp in the eastern suburbs of the city. After lying on the damp ground out there several days, I obtained permission to seek shelter at a residence somewhere in the vicinity. This change was necessary. I felt like my earthly career would end there if I did not get out of the camp.

I went to a good looking residence. A young lady came to the front gallery as I approached the house, and when I told her why I was there, she asked me to come in, and led the way into a room in which I arranged my blanket on the floor and laid down. After the first day in the house, she prepared a bed for me, which was much preferable to the floor, and made me feel better. She came frequently to ask my welfare and brought me something both palatable and nourishing to eat. I had no medicine, and of course, took none, but here treatment was much better than a physic.

This young lady was Miss Lou Winchester whose grandfather was the first mayor of Memphis. She was well educated and fully informed as to the cause of secession and was intensely Southern. I was well enough to walk in a few days but not strong enough for camp duty, when our regiment received orders to take the train for Corinth, Mississippi. Captain Cumby came for me and said we must go at once. Miss Lou interceded for me and obtained permission from the Captain to let her be the judge as to when I would be able to follow the regiment after it left Memphis.

Miss Lou was a brunette, a real beauty, a well read historian and fluent in conversation. I was so charmed that I listened much more than I tried to talk. There were two other sick soldiers in the house under her care. She treated us all alike, except that she talked more to me than the others. When I was convalescent we took frequent walks in the parks and other places of attraction in the city. I was then enjoying a real vacation from camp duty, but it couldn't last. I was there twelve days, the longest time out of camp that fell to my lot during the Lincoln war. When I felt strong enough to go to my regiment I told her that the pleasant time I was having under her care when sick, and with her, when convalescing, made me regret to have to say good-bye; but it couldn't be otherwise now, as I had to pay my board bill and catch the noon train. She would not accept any money from me, nor from the other two soldiers. She said I did not owe anything except a promise to come to see her if I should ever be at Memphis again. I could not say anything. I admired her devotion to 'our cause.' in nursing and aiding in restoration to health, the sick Confederate soldiers and enabling them to take their places again at the front, to resist invasion by the armed hosts who had come to destroy first the men, and then our Southland, to gratify the wishes and ambition of the fanatics who were in power. I could only take her offered hand in mine and try to say "Good-bye."

Arriving in Corinth I sought my regiment. Brother Rufus was a lieutenant in Company I, Nineteenth Louisiana Infantry, then in camp at Corinth, and he had been at the Third Texas Cavalry camp to see me but was told that I was left sick at Memphis. This was a disappointment to him besides making him uneasy about me. I obtained permission to visit him the next day. This was no small task. His division, brigade, regiment and company had all to be inquired before I found him. I had left him at Keachie, Louisiana in January 1861 when on my way to Henderson, Texas, and this was our first meeting since then.

I decided at once to ask for a transfer to his regiment. I wanted to be with him. My officers said they would sign an application for transfer, but did not like for me to leave the regiment because I had been with them since its organization in all its service up to this time. Association so long in the army and especially in as active service as we had been, draws men very closely to each other, and there forms a friendship which binds so strongly that only death can sever it. This good feeling towards me influenced my officers to grant my request. A battle was daily expected and I yielded to their wishes to remain until after the battle. However, the battle did not materialize. Gen. Grant was in command of the Federal army and was strongly fortifying Corinth, no doubt thinking the Confederates would attack him behind his breastworks; but in this, he was much mistaken.

CHAPTER XIX

HARDSHIPS — RETREAT
SICKNESS IN CAMP — DRILLING

Texas' General Albert Sydney Johnston's death at Shiloh, Tennessee, after a decided victory, caused it to be lost the next day. The deaths of Generals McCulloch and McIntosh at the battle of Pea Ridge, Arkansas on Friday morning, March 7th, 1862, caused the retreat of Gen. Van Dorn after he had gained a victory over the Federal army. As told in the preceding chapter, McCulloch was needed to direct his gallant division, which at that time, knew nothing about defeat, and any squad of five or ten men would have been glad to make the reconnoiter he was making personally when killed. McIntosh was killed while heading a charge to drive back the advancing Federals, when he was needed to direct that charge from a point at which his couriers could receive and deliver his orders. This is mentioned to show mistakes by brave and daring men who forget their true place in time of battle. We cannot censure them because those of us in private ranks who have felt that animated degree of courage and spirit of heroism, when forgetting danger, the thundering cannon and roar of musketry, we plunge forward to meet the advancing enemy, or to take a battery. Hence we can offer testimony on their behalf.

At Corinth the armies of the west under Van Dorn and Price were joined to those of Gens. Beauregard and Bragg. I have already told of the time and place when

Price's Missourians became Confederate soldiers. Disease, that fatal camp dysentery, attacked our armies at Corinth and we lost more men from it than we had lost in battle. We were looking for an attack by Gen. Grant which did not come to pass, and he was expecting an attack which we did not make.

Gen. Joseph L. Hogg, of Rusk, Texas, who had received a commission making him a brigadier general in the Confederate army, had arrived and our regiment was assigned to his brigade. When I learned he was in camp I went to see him. When I shook hands with him he said, "I knew that you were in the Third Texas and I have been wondering if you would come to see me. You came often to see me when in Rusk. I am glad to see you, sir." I said, "General you ought to know that I would come to see the man who proved to be a good friend to me, when I was a stranger just starting out from home on a new career. Tell me of your family and how you left them. I am sorry to find you sick." He told me about his family and when he left them. Poor man, he was on his death cot and lived only a week after I was with him. He had appointed our adjutant, M. D. Ector, his adjutant general, and Dr. Wallace McDugald of Company C, his brigade surgeon. After his death Gen. Cabell (old Tige) was assigned to our brigade.

When our first year's service was ended, the regiment was not allowed to return home nor to receive furloughs, but we were conscripted and given the privilege of re-enlisting for three years or the duration of the war, and we received orders to reorganize the regiment and elect officers. Mr. Rorrison told me that the 'boys' wanted me for one of the lieutenants. I told him that I appreciated this, but expected to forward my application to be transferred to the Nineteenth La. Infantry at once. I told him that I would go to work to secure a lieutenant's place for him, but wished he could go with me to the Nineteenth La. Infantry. He said, "We have been together a long time. I will not forget you and I hope you will live through this trouble we are in now."

The reorganization followed. Company B elected G. S. Boggess, Captain; Jessee Wynne, First Lieutenant; A. C. Rorrison Second Lieutenant; Taylor Brown, Third Lieutenant. The regiment elected our Captain Cumby to be colonel of the regiment, but he wanted to go home, so he resigned. This made a general change of officers necessary. I went to work in earnest for my personal friend Captain Jim Barker, who wanted to be major. The change resulted as follows: Col. Mabry; Lt. Col. Boggess; Major Jim Barker; Company B Captain, Jessee Wynne; First Lieutenant A. C. Rorrison; Second Lieutenant Taylor Brown; 3rd Lieutenant Rufus Childress. Our first adjutant, M. D. Ector, was elected colonel of the tenth Texas Regiment, and was promoted to the office of brigadier general before we left Corinth.

The lines of the Federal and Confederate armies were very near each other before we left that place. I was detailed one night to go on picket duty. Night changes of pickets were required on the east side of Corinth because of the nearness of the armies. No talking could be done unless at the risk of drawing the enemy's fire. It was a lonesome place and my thoughts had fair play. In the darkness I could hear the enemy picket clear his throat in a subdued or very low sound. No doubt he was a good soldier, obeying his country's call under the newly adopted plea of "Save the Flag and Preserve the Union" but really, as we of the South then believed, to emancipate the Negro from bondage and destroy The Southern confederacy, I too was obeying my country's call to resist invasion. I could think, in this lonesome but responsible position, but these thoughts were only to perish for naught.

American people needed wise men in control of national affairs in place of fanatics, who could see nothing but their own selfish wishes. Such was the situation for some time, before a separate government and divorce was contemplated, but this too never came to pass in full. There was division in sentiment in the seceded states just like that in the colonies who threw off English rule for American independence. There were always those who stood ready to aid the other side. No doubt the man behind a tree in that darkness, whom I could hear clear his throat with as little sound as possible, was thinking, too; perhaps, of home and mother, or perhaps of wife and children or of "the girl I left behind me," and wishing there were some way to settle differences other than with cannon and musket or sword. And the president in Washington might be thinking, too, "What a great name I am getting, by my plan of action," when in his disturbed slumbers on his downy pillow, he awakes to meditate. Meanwhile, this lonesome "Fed" and I were watching each other for a chance to send a deadly missile into the other's heart to end his soldiership. But such is war. I was glad when

another man came in the darkness and whispered, "I
have come to relieve you."

Not many days after this I was among the victims of
camp dysentery. Early one morning Capt. Wynne came
to my tent and said. "You are sick, let Willis Poe have
your gun." I said, "Captain, please do not insist on
Willis' having my gun. Take him along with you without
a gun; if you get in a skirmish he will come in tonight
without a gun. That is his record, first to throw away his
gun and then to seek a place of safety." "No, Cater" he
said, "Let Willis have your gun, and I'll get you another
gun if yours is lost. You must stay in your tent today."
I let Willis have my gun but he returned without it. He
had thrown it away. I was not in a good humor with
either Capt. Wynne or Willis Poe. My gun was a nice
one and I wanted to send it home if an opportunity ever
came, or keep it and take it home with me if living. I
knew that all wars have to end. Wynne obtained
another gun for me, but I left it with the regiment later
when my transfer came back to me approved.

Gen. Price commanded our forces at the Battle of
Farmington and was successful. On our return to camp
after this victory, I was too sick to stay with the regiment. I was not well when we left camp that morning
but I wanted to go, and did go. I had to lie down on the
roadside and remain there alone all night, but was able
the next day to get back to camp. Lieut. Col. Walter P.
Lane was left out at our reorganization of the regiment,
but had not gone home at the time of the Battle of
Farmington, and Col. Mabry, through courtesy, had
asked him to command the regiment that day. On

leaving the battlefield, Lane saw a brigade of Federals which had been formed in line to protect the retreat of the Federal army. Without orders from General Price or anybody else, he ordered our regiment to charge that Federal brigade. The regiment was repulsed with the loss of some of our best men, and among them my loved friend Major Barker. Col. Lane made a very grave mistake. He was brave enough to have been a good private soldier, but was out of place as an officer, and yet, he was made a brigadier general in the Trans-Mississippi Department after he returned home from Corinth.

The continued dysentery among our soldiers was decimating our ranks to such an extent that we were ordered to leave Corinth and move south to Tupelo. My transfer having come back approved, I went to my brother and became a member of Company I, Nineteenth Louisiana Infantry at Tupelo.

The horses belonging to the men of the Third Texas Cavalry which had been sent from Duvall's Bluff on White River, Arkansas to Texas, were brought back to them soon after I left the regiment, and Professor Mitchell rode my horse after my transfer.

It is impossible for me to tell how glad I was to be with brother Rufus again. When I was a boy I looked up to him. His influence was for good only. I had always loved him and when we were soldiers together this love had matured almost into idolatry.

The Nineteenth La. Infantry was a part of Gen. Dan Adams' brigade. He was a colonel at the Battle of Shiloh and received a wound in his head and one eye, and was lying in a mud hole when some soldiers passing, saw him. One of them said, "Here is a big officer, but he is dead and we will have to leave him." Adams, hearing what was said, called to them as they were leaving and said, "Men, if you will wash some of this mud off my face I will feel better." They were glad to hear him speak and gave him all the assistance they could. He was taken to a field hospital and afterwards to a better place where he recovered, but carried an ugly scar and lost his wounded eye. He was made a brigadier general when he was able to return to duty. We were at Tupelo several weeks and time was spent in drilling. The men needed rest and better food. The drill could not give this, but if Gen. Bragg ever did anything right, I never heard of it. There were so many sick men in the army that the regiments, brigades and divisions, were made up of fragments of the different commands for the drill. It took part of three companies of our regiment to make a company of 100 men. Ambulances were sent with the different brigades to take the men to camp, who fell out of ranks from weakness while drilling, and these ambulances would be filled with weak and exhausted men. On one occasion there was a review. A letter to Cousin Em tells about it. I tried to make a good picture of it and other things. The letter was preserved and came to my hands after her death, and I copy it here in this little volume.

Camp near Tupelo, Miss. July 22,1862

Miss M. Em Reagan
New Salem, Rusk County, Texas.

Dear "Cousin" Em:

How anxiously impatient I am, waiting to hear from you again! The long sultry summer days come and go, weeks roll away, and months are added to the calendar of the past; yet it seems that no little white winged messenger will come to break the monotony of camp life and tell of the welfare of the absent loved ones. I am often lonely not-with-standing the noise and often calls and moves of the army. Still, I find pleasure in the discharge of my military duties, but that pleasure is chiefly derived from love of country and from the sanguine hope that my humble efforts will in some measure contribute to the consummation most devoutly to be wished, the independence of the Southern States. But my thoughts are often amid other scenes, and dreams transport me to happier associations. In rainbow beauty, the past is often vivid before me. But I am aroused from the intoxicating reveries; the elusive dream is dispelled with its magic visions of loveliness by the rugged realities of the returning dawn. The picture fades away like 'twilight on the waters of the blue.' And yet, ever and anon, amid the changing scenes through which I pass, these visions return. Let fate do her worst, there are moments of joy. Bright dreams of the past, which cannot dim, which come in the night time of sorrow and care, and bring back the features that joy used to wear. Long, long, be my heart with such memories filled. Like the vase in which roses have once been distilled. You may break, you may shatter the vase if you will, but the scent of the roses will hang 'round it still.

Our Division (Jones') was reviewed a few mornings since by Major General Hardee, the present commander of the 2nd Corps, as Gen. Bragg, its former commander, had succeeded General Beauregard in the command of the Western Department. We were paraded in an old field where the view was unobstructed and the long lines of troops with arms bright and bayonets gleaming, the soul stirring strains of martial music from the splendid regimental bands and the proud banners unfurled to the morning breeze, gave the scene an interest deep and touching. Such a scene is seldom, if ever, witnessed by those in the walks of civil or peaceful life, and reminded me of the description of King James' army, "'Twas worth ten years of peaceful life to see that grand array." Gen. Bragg was present. From a gentle eminence the veteran chief mounted on his war horse and surrounded by his staff scanned with eagle eye the moving columns. But others were there who honored us with their presence. My bosom thrilled with strange emotions as I beheld them. And think you these were some statesmen grave, and whose burning eloquence had often enchained a listening, spellbound Senate. No, not they. Some warriors then, men of renown, whose deeds have been the theme of inspiration to the bard or have shone with luster bright on the pages of the historian. No, none of these. 'Twas woman, lovely woman! They had come out from their peaceful, vine clad homes to witness the review. While we have the approving smiles of the fair daughters of the South, while their prayers, pure as the breath of Heaven, ascend to the Supreme for blessings to rest upon us, while they look to use for defense and protection, shall we never lay down our arms at the feet of our foe and suffer him to bind us with his chains. Welcome first the grave.

How grateful we should be that victory has again perched upon the Confederate banner! McClellan with his proud hosts marching "to destroy Richmond and capture the entire Rebel Army" has been somewhat impeded in his progress. He was driven back thirty miles and was at last sheltered by his gun boats in the James River. Then Richmond was not taken nor destroyed. But President Lincoln seems yet to have hope of our subjugation and has ordered out 300,000 more men to take the field. Let them come on, we will welcome them to hospitable graves. Many of us have to lie down in the dust, yet our slumber will be sweet for we shall have died in a just and holy cause. I am with my brother Rufus in the 19th La. Regiment of Infantry. Our mutual sympathies, wishes and affections rendered his companion- ship most desirable and as we are far from home and kindred, far from all beloved and all who loved us, you must know that we find pleasure in each others society of an exalted nature. I have had no letters from home across the Mississippi in a long time. Nothing either from my brother Wade at Vicksburg of recent date. I trust, however, that 'all is well.' It is rumored and believed that we will move soon. I do not know to what point we will go. If true, I shall be deprived the pleasure of reading a favor from you soon. Good-bye. May all that is desirable be yours, is the sincere wish of your friend.

Douglas J. Cater

CHAPTER XX

HEALTH REGAINED
SIX MONTHS IN ONE CAMP

On August 2nd, 1862, our regiment received orders to take the railroad train at Tupelo, which was going south. I lost sight of the main army and cannot tell what disposition was made of it for the next six months and will only write of our regiment and my experience during this time. Arriving at Mobile we left the train and took passage on a steamboat which carried us to Montgomery. On this steamboat I met Matt Gayle, a first cousin of my mother's. He was not connected with the army at that time and was returning home from a business trip to Mobile. He later became a colonel in the army. After a short stay at Montgomery where we left the steamboat, we again went on a train which took us to Pollard, our destination.

We went into camp and I learned we had been sent there to guard Pensacola, Florida, which was only fifty miles distant, if it became necessary to use us. At Pollard we were supplied with an abundance of sweet potatoes and on this simple diet every man in the regiment was entirely cured of that plague, 'camp dysentery,' which had so decimated our army at Corinth and Tupelo. Drilling and dress parades were our main duties at Pollard. Of course, guard duty was never left off.

In September I obtained my first leave of absence.

This was a seven day furlough, too limited to allow a visit home, so I used it in visiting relatives, some at Burnt Corn, and some friends of my father at Sparta, all in Conecuh County, Alabama. I was born in Sparta twenty-one years before this visit, and I wanted to see the old town. Had I been a king instead of a private soldier in the Confederate army, I could not have been treated more royally while on this seven day furlough. On the first night when shown my room, I had lain down in the soft bed which had been prepared for me, and pulling the clean white sheet over me I said, "Too good for a soldier." A rap on the door, when the sun was shining brightly an hour high the next morning, and a voice saying "Get ready for breakfast!" awoke me. The rap and voice were that of Cousin Lawrence Cater, a lieutenant in his company, who was on furlough and was visiting his family, a wife and two children, at the home of his father-in-law Judge Green, at Burnt Corn. Cousin Lawrence was the son of Uncle Edwin Cater, my father's oldest brother, living then at Marshall, Texas. He was First Lieutenant E. L. Cater in a company and regiment of Florida cavalry. His home was at Milton, Florida. I went with him the next day in a deer drive. There was an extra gun in the house which was furnished me. I shot at a deer but it was beyond the range of the gun and ran on unharmed.

The seven day furlough was soon ended and the pleasures of the trip all in the past. When I returned to Pollard I learned that I had been promoted. Colonel Winans, commander of the regiment had concluded to have a band of four drummers. He had made me drum

major. We had one drummer and the colonel appointed two more private soldiers, which made four,
and we went to work with the drums he had bought for
us. He knew that I was a musician because I was called
that in my transfer to his regiment, but I had never
learned to beat a drum. He told me that he needed a
band for roll call, dress parade and drilling. This
relieved me of musket and guard duty, but I had to rise
early because my band was needed for reveille to wake
up the soldiers in the early dawn, and this had to be
regular. But I met all these requirements and soon had
a good drum band. The 'long roll' was the hardest for
me to learn. It meant fall into line for battle. At dress
parade the regiment in line stood at attention. The
band's duty was to pass in front, keeping step with the
drum beats in slow marching time, 'till reaching the
head of the column; then about face and return at
'quick step' with beats arranged for that purpose.

Our camp was getting dull and monotonous when
someone proposed that a string band be organized, if
there were enough musicians in the regiment to form a
good orchestra. A purse was made up and sent to
Mobile for musical instruments. We secured a good
violin, a guitar, a bass violin and a piccolo (an octave
keyed flute). The violin was given to brother Rufus, the
guitar to John Bonham, the bass violin to Lieut. Frank
Smith and the piccolo to me. These were all members
of Company I except John Bonham. Brother Rufus was
first lieutenant of the company. It was not long before
we had a good orchestra and were having good music.
Col. Winans was a lover of music and seemingly en-

joyed our music better than anyone else. This was encouraging to us. All the regiment loved Col. Winans and he was worthy of it. One of our selections we called 'Col. Winans' Favorite' because it was his favorite among all our pieces. John Bonham was a good singer and had many songs in store which the other members of the band soon learned and we formed a quartet. There were some good families in Pollard while we were there. Some of them were refugees from Mobile, Pensacola and Milton. They were sometimes serenaded with songs and solos and we were always rewarded with a nice treat, wine and cake, and sometimes with more substantial viands. Mr. LeBaron from Mobile with his family, had a charming daughter, Miss Addie, who often repaid us with good music on the piano. During the winter, Lieutenant Henry Ivey of Company A told the members of our band that his wife was on a visit to Lowndes County and that she had written to him that she would come to see him and bring four young ladies, relatives, with her to stay a week, if he would prepare a cabin to stay in while in camp. We told him to write to her that the house would be ready. We helped him to build it, and carpeted the dirt floor with pine straw. and helped him make camp stools and benches, tables and shelves for brushes, combs and little mirrors. When finished and thus furnished this little cabin looked really nice to us soldiers.

Mrs. Ivey came, and with her the promised young ladies, and they remained a week. They were Misses Tennie, Bamma and Daught Gordon and Miss Clara, sister of Judge John B. Haralson of Selma. Miss Clara

had a splendid voice and gave us some good music with
her guitar, which she brought with her. Our orchestra
contributed as much as we could to their entertainment. Miss Addie LeBaron gave them an entertainment, to which she invited the other young ladies at
Pollard. Col. Winans, Major Butler, Captains Handley
and Pearson, Lieut. Ivey and wife and Sergeant Prude,
the members of our orchestra, and some others of the
regiment. I think this entertainment was one of their
most enjoyed evenings of their 'stay' in camp. Some
lasting friendships were formed during that short week,
but I can tell of them later.

Col. Winans gave me a few days leave of absence
during the Christmas week. I went to Sparta and spent
one night with Col. John D. Cary, an old neighbor and
friend of my father before my family moved to Texas.
He told me of many pleasant days spent with him, and
of their many deer drives. He thought father was the
best shot at a deer and the best rider on horseback he
ever saw. Miss Kate, his fascinating daughter, took me
on a pleasant drive in the buggy the next day. I went
one afternoon to Evergreen to see my father's oldest
sister, Mrs. Eliza McPherson, her two daughters and
two grand-daughters. From Evergreen I went to Burnt
Corn. Cousin Lawrence Cater had been called from
the army to the senate in Tallahassee, Florida, and was
with his family at Judge Green's, preparing to assume
his new duties. I returned to Pollard and my first act
was to thank Col. Winans for the pleasures he had
permitted me to enjoy during the Yuletide, with friends
and relatives away from camp.

The mild days of February had induced Col. Winans to plant a garden at Pollard. The vegetables were growing nicely. The clear running water in the Escambia River was inviting and every day found some soldiers enjoying a plunge and swim. Of course I was with them when other duties were not calling me. The fish were hungry and we had many meals of fried fish, which were enjoyed as a change from the beef steaks allotted to us from the butcher pen across the river from our camp. Our regiment was basking in the nice sunshine. The balmy days of spring had come and we welcomed them although the winter had been mild. With us it was springtime. The growing green grass and the green leaves of the trees sheltering it on the banks of Little Escambia were first to entice us to try the hook and line for the red perch and cunning bass to add to our 'rations.' A springboard plunge was much enjoyed by those who loved to swim. Our garden was yielding bountifully in rich nourishing vegetables, but all this must end, and end at once.

The Mobile *Register* had suggested that Col. Winans' example in raising vegetables during the winter for the soldiers, should be appreciated and imitated. Gen. Braxton Bragg either saw this or remembered when we were sent, and decided he had a better use for us and that Pensacola was not liable to be attacked, at least in the near future. Forthwith, there came an order for us to rejoin the brigade at once. Of course we obeyed orders and prepared for a long journey and for a very different climate. Our first stop was at Mobile Camp, which we left on April 15th on a steamboat enroute to

Montgomery. We passed Selma and stopped one night at Montgomery.

This city has its memories. It was the first capital of the Confederate States of America as a government, born in February, 1861. I have mentioned this in a previous chapter. It was not prepared for war and there was hope that there would be none. Now there was no prospect for peace, but there was determination on the part of the citizen soldiery to repel the invading hosts of the president in Washington.

CHAPTER XXI

I FIND BROTHER WADE'S GRAVE
VICKSBURG FALLS

We left Montgomery April 18th on the train and arrived at Atlanta, Georgia on the same date. We left Atlanta on the 19th and arrived that evening at Chattanooga, Tennessee. It was not springtime here and we felt seriously the difference in temperature from that of Alabama. Our conveyance now was by freight trains in box cars and open flat cars. Brother Rufus and I, with many others, rode on top of a box car. We slept some up there, but our blankets, clothes and faces were covered with black cinders from the smoke of the engine. My! My! We were a sight when we came down from the top of that car. We left Chattanooga on the 20th and arrived at Tullahoma in the evening. We passed through a wild mountainous region, so different from the level pine woods of southern Alabama where we had, in some measure, enjoyed the past winter. At Tullahoma we left the cars and marched out one mile to the camp of our brigade. The 'boys' received us with shouting and cheers. Some wag said, "Hey, you Pollard gardeners, glad to see you!" The Mobile papers had published something about our nice garden at Pollard.

On April 24th, our brigade marched to Wartrace, a distance of ten miles. We crossed Duck River which we had to wade. The water was swift, clear and cold and about knee deep. Nature had paved the bed of the river with rocks or sharp edged stones which hurt our feet. We had pulled off our shoes and socks and had rolled up our pants above the knees, a ludicrous picture, but no serious accident occurred. We bivouacked on the clear, purling stream under beech trees which were budding, soon to give a dense shade. On our right a little green clover meadow in the valley suggesting a place for drilling and on our left was a hill rising high and abrupt, rugged with rocks. Brother Rufus was detailed to go with twenty men to have the wagons loaded with our baggage, which indicated a stay of several days at that place. Together we attended church on Sabbath, May 3d, at a beautiful Presbyterian Church in the country. We drilled the next two days. On the 6th our brigade marched eight miles through mud and rain to Beech Grove, near Hoover's Gap. The next day was cold with rain. Brother Rufus was quite sick with fever and headache. May 10th was Sabbath but not a rest day. We had to march several miles to be reviewed. Drilling filled the balance of the week. On the 21st, our regiment, Nineteeth La., drilled against the Fourth Kentucky Infantry. Generals Breckenridge, Adams and Helm, complimented us for efficiency in the drill, both officers and men. I took a part in this drill and beat good time on the drum for the 'boys' and they won. The Kentuckians acknowledged that they were beaten fairly.

On May 22d our regiment was sent to Hoover's Gap, four miles distant, on picket duty. We were alarmed about 11:00 A.M. by a raid of Federal cavalry who had flanked our cavalry pickets, killing one man and capturing one lieutenant and six men. They came near enough for us to see the dust of the cavalcade, and then retired. They had a battery and had done some cannon shooting in our direction, which had been replied to, on the road they were coming, and when we were passing a house on this road an old lady came out of it, wringing her hands and said to us, "I didn't mind them little guns, but them cannon, them cannon!"

Gen. Bragg commanded that part of the army and was needing every available man to face the Federal army, but Gen. Pemberton, who had disobeyed the orders of Gen. Johnston, to leave Vicksburg and come to him and was sustained in this disobedience by President Davis, was needing reinforcements at Vicksburg against the advance of General Grant.

Gen. Joseph E. Johnston had been sent to command the Department of the West. He had ordered Pemberton to evacuate Vicksburg, because to send troops from Bragg's army in Tennessee to aid Pemberton would cripple Bragg's army, and not help Pemberton. Johnston knew that if Pemberton remained in Vicksburg, he would not only lose the place, but his army also, but the War Department and President Davis were never known during the entire war to accede to the generalship of Joseph E. Johnston. On the contrary, they threw every possible impediment to frustrate his plans and prevent his success. This was a great help to Mr. Lincoln in the destruction of the Confederate States government.

Gen. Johnston was instructed to order troops from Bragg's army in Tennessee to Jackson, Mississippi, for

Pemberton's relief. So on May 23d our brigade struck tents and marched to Wartrace where we got on freight cars bound southward. We passed through Chattanooga, Atlanta, West Point and Montgomery, to Tensas landing and there got on a steamboat for Mobile. After passing West Point the cars stopped a little while in a large plantation near the railroad and where the cars stopped, some Negroes were cooking dinner for the 'field hands.' Three large kettles filled with cowpeas were just ready for eating. These were too tempting to be passed unnoticed by hungry soldiers whose appetites were just then ready to appreciate a dinner of well cooked and well seasoned peas. I was among those who, climbing down from the car, ran to those kettles. The engineer whistled to start when we had about half finished the unexpected but appreciated lunch. At Mobile we again went on freight cars enroute to the northwest. We passed Meridian, Mississippi, and arrived at the end of the railroad four miles from Jackson. The Federals had captured Jackson and destroyed the railroad that far out, when they left.

On May 31st we marched to Jackson and bivouacked near the city. On June 1st we pitched tents in a valley about 200 yards from the Capitol. Our regiment was on picket duty three miles from town on the evening and night of June 3d, but returned to camp on the 4th.

The next day brother Rufus and I, after a long search in the cemetery at this place, found the grave of our dear brother Wade, which was marked by a plain board with his name and the number of his regiment. He was a member of the Twenty-Seventh Louisiana Infantry, then in the trenches at Vicksburg. He had contracted cold in the trenches and was sent out to Jackson, where he died. We found a marble slab in an old marble yard and cut his name, age and regiment on it and placed it at the head of his grave. Many soldiers were sleeping around, like him, buried by strangers. But it was a quiet peaceful place. No more battles nor storms of life; he sleeps. His life up to the beginning of the war had been one of pleasure to his parents, brothers and sisters; a gentle, sweet, obedient child to his parents and companion to brothers and sisters, but his life was sacrificed in defence of the home that our chief enemy was seeking to destroy, an offer on the altar of his ambition.

Up to the time of our arrival in Jackson, Colonel Winans had ordered that the instruments of our string band have transportation with the baggage of the regiment, and they were again called into requisition while we were encamped in the capital of Mississippi. Our band went out in an ambulance one beautiful moonlight night, 3-1/2 miles from town, to serenade some young ladies. Our adjutant, Ben Broughton, Capt. Hodges, Sergeant Prude and the members of our band made a party of seven in the ambulance. The home we serenaded was a neat country seat embosomed in shrubbery and flowers. After a few pieces of music, candles were brought, and the folding doors thrown open by an affable old gentleman, who welcomed us and invited us into the dining room where a sumptuous repast awaited us. Flowers in midst, floating islands, cake which brother Rufus said "was too pretty to cut," wines, salads and too much more to mention were all there for us. The vase in the center of the table was inscribed "Vicksburg, Vicksburg, Vicksburg." Dainty notes were half concealed amid the flowers, thanking us for the serenade and conveying happy wishes, etc.

General Joseph E. Johnston had personal command of the little army at Jackson, and finding that Gen. Pemberton had determined not to evacuate Vicksburg and come to him, was gathering a force to go to Pemberton, who was now nearly surrounded by Grant's Army. Hence the name Vicksburg on the flower vase at the home of these young ladies which, should Vicksburg fall, would soon be desecrated by Federal soldiers. Somebody had told these young ladies of our proposed serenade, and the splendid supper awaited us to show their appreciation and to encourage us while defending their home.

We received an invitation to spend an evening at the home of a Miss Dickson and her grandmother. Miss Dickson was a musician and played the piano, guitar and violin. Our band cheerfully accepted the invitation and had planned for a musical treat, but the evening we expected to spend at that home three miles from Jackson was spent in preparation for a march towards Vicksburg.

We marched to Clinton July 1st and bivouacked southeast of the town; then marched to Bolton, a depot on U.S. and T. Railroad, on July 2d. The weather was very hot and the dust almost suffocating. We remained at Bolton until the morning of July 5th, and I slept on a bench in a church house. It was a hard bed. We left Bolton on July 5th and marched six miles to Springs, near the battlefield of Baker's Creek, and bivouacked for the night. Here we got news of the fall of Vicksburg. We then left camp near Baker's Creek and returned to Bolton. Gloom is on every countenance, with Pemberton's army prisoners in the hands of Gen. Grant and the war prolonged. Had Pemberton obeyed orders and brought his army to General Johnston, we would have defeated Grant before his reinforcements came to him. Flushed with victory in the fall of Vicksburg and the surrender of Pemberton's army, Grant rushed to engulf Johnston. It looked so easy. But he knew that Joseph E. Johnston had no superior as a general and supreme caution would be necessary even with his great superiority of numbers over Johnston's little band of Confederates falling back to Jackson.

CHAPTER XXII

PLAYING A PIANO IN THE TRENCHES
WHILE THE ENEMY CHARGES

Our regiment left Bolton at 1:00 A.M. and made a circuitous march to Jackson covering a distance of twenty-two miles, stopping once to cook rations and another to do picket duty. Gen. Johnston had taken the precaution to have the breastworks strengthened at Jackson. Our regiment took position in rear of the breastworks. We were aroused at 3:00 A.M. on July 9th and took position in the trenches.

On the 10th a call was made for volunteers to sharpshoot in front of our position. I volunteered to go and a musket and cartridges were furnished me. There were five of us in the squad. We took position in a clump of trees not far from Col. Cooper's residence. This was a fine two story house. His family had moved out but had left their furniture, carpets, mirrors and a fine piano. There was a large cistern under a dwelling in the yard. The water was cool and it seemed that the Federals knew that cistern of good water was there and they wanted it. Their guns were better than ours and they were doing good execution while our guns could not reach them, only raise the dust twenty or thirty feet in front of them. One of our squad, a young man nineteen years old, was shot in the leg breaking a bone below the knee. Poor fellow! He called loudly for Mama. We had to let two of our squad take him to the breastworks. The enemy saw this and doubled their fire on us. We had found that our guns were doing no damage and as there were only two of us now, we protected ourselves behind trees. We could not be relieved until after dark. I told the 'boys' I would not volunteer to sharpshoot anymore if I could not get a longer ranging gun. But that position attracted so much attention that Gen. Johnston ordered the house to be burned. I went back there with others after nightfall before the torch was applied and carried away a little piece of broken mirror and about a yard of Brussells carpet for use in camp. Some men from Slocumb's Battery took the piano to the breastworks. Our regiment was just on the right of this battery facing the enemy. The piano was near the cannon but was protected by the breastworks. Gen. Grant was trying to outflank us and get possession of Pearl River on our left and east of town. There were repeated efforts or charges on our right. We could witness the charge and repulse of the enemy. They succeeded in placing a battery in front of our position, but we were protected by the breastworks. Captain Slocumb was too wise to reply and thus give them knowledge of his position.

On the 12th of July they decided, after much shelling, to take our breastworks. Some of our regiment had told the battery 'boys' to send for me and that I would give them some good music on that piano. Slocumb sent for me, and brother Rufus went with me. We were enjoying the music, paying no attention to the shells and minnie balls which were passing over us when Capt. Slocumb, standing near the piano, caught the sound of the Federal yell, and looking over the breastworks, saw them coming on a charge. He was at his guns and brother Rufus and I were back at our posts with the regiment quicker than the time it has taken to write of this incident. We had reserved our fire until Slocumb's Battery opened fire on them. It seems that this was the signal for an attack all along the line but it met with such fearful slaughter that they retired out of the range of our guns.

Our brigade commander Gen. Dan Adams, mounted the breastworks and fired two rounds with a musket of one of our company men. Such is the indescribable enthusiasm which drives out fear in the storm of battle and sometimes causes our best generals to forget that too much depends on them to take such risks. Gen. Scott once said of Joseph E. Johnston, "A good officer, but confound the fellow, he always gets shot!" We took 150 prisoners in front of our brigade, who would not attempt to fall back under the fire of our muskets. After the firing ceased and quiet was restored, I went back to the piano and we had more music.

In two days the stench of dead men was so great that an armistice of several hours was agreed to, that we might bury the enemy's dead. One hundred sixty were counted a short distance from Slocumb's Battery and our regiment in front of our breastworks. This number added to the 150 prisoners and 160 wounded made a loss of 570 from the division that charged us. We did not lose any men on this occasion.

Slocumb said, when we went back to the piano to have more music, that he was afraid when he got to his guns that he had let them (the Federals) get too close to stop them. But he had a bag of buckshot rammed down for the first load and when he saw the effect of that first shot, he felt safe.

Col. Cooper gave that piano to Slocumb's Battery at New Orleans a few years after the war ended. Jackson was not a strategic point because of its easy liability to be flanked. General Johnston kept Grant in check long enough to get the government stores he had accumulated there safely away and then decided a surprise for Grant who had planned a complete rout or capture of Johnston's little army. We silently decamped on the night of July 16th and marched to Brandon, fifteen miles from Jackson. On the 17th our regiment, with one section of the Washington Artillery, went to guard the main road in the rear of one wing of the army. We were in line of battle all night.

On July 18th we marched seventeen miles in clouds of dust; and the weather was very hot. In the evening the rain fell in torrents, but we continued our march through mud and water until we came to our wagon park. Clothes and blankets were saturated, and the rain was still pouring. But we succeeded in building fires and partially drying our clothes. Then with a cold biscuit and a cup of poor coffee for supper, brother Rufus and I laid down on the wet ground and slept: for we were tired and sleepy as we had slept none scarcely for three nights. By July 19th we were on Line Creek, five miles from Mortin Station. The sun was shining through broken clouds when we awoke. We left this camp on July 21st and marched five or six miles east of

Mortin Station to a camp in the woods. The weather was very hot with an occasional rain. Brother Rufus and I stretched one of our blankets over a pole resting across two small forks and thus furnished a pretty good place to sleep. We had a cook while in camp. Our rations at that place were cornmeal and fresh beef without bacon or lard. We also had roasting ears; three per man were issued to us. Here brother Rufus obtained a leave of absence and went to Alabama for a few days.

Gen. Johnston was relieved and Gen. Bragg placed in command. There was nothing of importance after Bragg assumed command while we were in this region. The army was divided and in the latter part of August our division (then Breckinridge's) was ordered to Chattanooga, Tennessee. The part of the army which had not been sent to Jackson, Mississippi was in this vicinity, having fallen back from where we had left it to go to Jackson, Mississippi. A part of it was at Knoxville under command of General Buckner, and the cavalry force was at Rome, Georgia.

The Federals, commanded by Gen. Rosecrans, were advancing, having crossed the mountains and taken Cumberland Gap in their advance. The main forces crossed the Tennessee River at Bridgeport and Stevenson, in order to flank us. They were coming by way of Lafayette and Ringgold. Our division had left Chattanooga and was again with the main army.

Gen. Longstreet's corps of the Virginia army was sent to reinforce our army. They had arrived and we were very much encouraged because we certainly needed more men. Some of Longstreet's men said they had come over to show us how to fight. We told them we were glad to have them with us, but they would find quite a difference in facing these western men from those they had been fighting in Virginia. They acknowledged this before they were sent back to General Lee. We were expecting the Federals to attack us from the mountain gorges and our trains and supplies were sent to the rear and our army concentrated along the Chickamauga Creek. Our (Breckinridge's) division was now in General Polk's corps. This was Bishop Polk of the Methodist Church, South.

CHAPTER XXIII

BATTLE OF CHICKAMAUGA
I BURY BROTHER RUFUS

On Friday evening Gen. Walker's division had a skirmish at Alexander's Bridge. The enemy fell back and destroyed the bridge but a ford was found and crossed after nightfall. So did Gen. Hood's division. The next morning, September 19th, Walker's, Hood's, Cheatham's and Stewart's divisions were all engaged and the battle continued all day with successes and losses and at night nothing had been gained and the troops slept on their arms on the battlefield. Generals Forrest and Wheeler with their cavalry command checked and prevented flank movements. Brother Rufus had returned from his pleasant trip to Alabama and had gathered information that our army was to be organized as two corps, Longstreet's and Polk's.

While in Alabama he had visited Miss Clara Haralson, one of the young ladies who had contributed so much to the pleasure of our regiment by their presence and music on their visit with Lieut. Henry's wife at Pollard when we were in winter quarters there. He told me also that he and Miss Clara had plighted vows and would be married after the end of the war. Then he said to me, "My dear brother please grant me one request. We will be in line of battle early on tomorrow morning and no doubt ordered to charge the enemy. You are the drum major of the regiment and are required to go

with us in a charge. Will you please not go?" I told him
I would work in the infirmary corps and assist in taking
care of the wounded. He said there was no safe place
on a battlefield in an engagement and he hoped I would
stay out of danger. I told him I would try but would
much rather be with him.

Gen. Polk commanding the right was to attack the
enemy at daylight and General Longstreet the left. The
order to our regiment was to be ready to move at
daylight Sunday morning September 20th, 1863, and we
were ready. We received no orders to move until the
sun was over an hour high. I learned afterwards that
Gen. Polk waited until after a late breakfast before
ordering his troops to move forward. By this time the
enemy were in the position that we were expected to
take at daylight. It was about ten o'clock when in line
of battle, we were ordered to charge. Brother Rufus
repeated his request to me not to go with them in the
charge. He was in command of our company. I stopped
but the regiment moved forward at double quick. The
enemy was shelling us when the order came. The regiment was soon out of my sight in the brush and I knew
from the roar of musketry and the cheering, that they
started after the battery that had been shelling us.
Pretty soon Malvern Collins, a private in our company
came limping up to where I was and asked me to carry
him to the field hospital. He had been shot in the hip.
By using his musket for support he had limped that far,
but could go no farther. He had no use of one of his
legs. I succeeded in getting him to a place where the
surgeons had stopped with an ambulance, and returned

to where I last saw my regiment, and met them coming back; but brother Rufus was not with them. Mr. Hinson, a member of the regiment, but not of my company, saw me and said Lieutenant Cater fell in front of his company just before we got to the battery. "We could not hold it because of the deadly infantry fire which was directed at us from behind it. As we were falling back I passed Lieutenant Cater, who raising himself on his elbow said, 'Good-bye boys,' and fell back." I could not go to him then, the enemy held that part of the battlefield. I was one of four men who then carried a Mr. Braden, a soldier of the regiment, on a stretcher a half mile or more to a field hospital. I fainted from fatigue and heat but returned to the regiment. The enemy's main strength seemed to be against our corps.

About four o'clock in the evening another general assault was made and this time the enemy was driven from all of the positions gained in the morning, and before nightfall Rosecrans' army was in full retreat toward Chattanooga. I hastened to the place where our regiment made the charge in the morning. This was Snodgrass Hill. I found some others there looking for missing relatives and friends. We found the bodies of Major Butler, Captain Handley, Lieut. Williams, and Matt Hendrick. Continuing my search I met my old friend Jack Franks who had found Brother Rufus' body and was looking for me. He led the way and soon I was beside the lifeless form of my dear brother. His blanket which he had folded in the morning and carried over his shoulder, the ends tied with a string at his side, had been unfolded and he was lying on it, cold in death. His watch, his purse, the shoes from his feet, his sword and scabbard had all been taken. His pants pockets were turned wrong side out, and the devils in human form, not yet satisfied, had fired a rifle ball through his forehead. The ball which caused him to fall in the charge had passed through his breast and out at his back through the folds of his blanket, but not near his heart. He might had gotten well of this wound, but the ball through his forehead was sufficient evidence that he was murdered while a prisoner on the battlefield. Near him was a wounded Federal soldier, a foreigner who could not speak our language plainly, but could say water, and for this he was begging. I could not resist handing him my canteen which was about one third full. He placed it to his mouth and when he gave it back to me there was not a drop in it. He said nothing, but went to sleep. He was not fighting for flag nor country but was a hireling in the ranks of our enemies. Yet he was a human being in distress and I gave him what he asked for, not knowing when nor where my canteen could be refilled. But what of the grand man, the patriot, the hero, the brother, the son, the martyr in gray uniform who had answered the last roll call, who had given his life in defense of home, of mother, of Southern rights, of Southern honor, of State, of Country! This was to be my last night with brother Rufus and yet I was not to be with him for he was gone. This was his cold still body. All my sweet associations were in now in the eternal past. With my arms around this lifeless form, sleep came to this tired soldier. When I awoke the sun was shining in my face. During the night the Federal soldier had died. His corpse was lying near me when I awoke. I went to the regiment who had slept on their arms nearby, and were now at breakfast. They had orders to move forward expecting to encounter the Federals, not knowing that they were at that time not only on the retreat but crossing the Tennessee River at Chattanooga to get out of danger. When the regiment was ready to move forward a detail of men was left to go to the wagons for spades and picks to bury our dead. Dr. Gus Hendrick, a private in our company, obtained a spade and pick and he and I dug two graves, one for his brother and one for mine. It took a long time and much hard work to get these graves ready. We wrapped blankets around the bodies of our brothers and placed them in these crude graves. There were no caskets, no flowers, but there were loving hands that filled in the earth on these blanket enshrouded forms and cut their names on the rough boards which marked 'the place where they were laid.' There were sad bleeding hearts and there were falling tears which helped us to bear the pains of loss and separation.

Our regiment met no opposing foe. No stop was made by the enemy until they arrived in Chattanooga. Our army did not press a further engagement. Gen. Dan Adams who was captured when our brigade made the charge on Sunday morning, said afterwards that he had hoped and expected a renewed attack on September 21st by Gen. Bragg as it would have resulted in either a rout or capture of Gen. Rosecrans' army. But Bragg was not like Stonewall Jackson, nor Gen. McIntosh who was killed at Pea Ridge, Arkansas in 1862.

This was his first and only complete victory. He never did anything to merit the love of his soldiers, but much to make them dislike him. We were reviewed in a few days by Gen. Bragg and President Davis, the only time I ever saw our president. He would have been a splendid president in time of peace because he was a statesman, but not a strategist in time of war. Had the armies of the United States and the Confederate States been equal in numbers of men, of course, a different history would have been written.

Our cooks were with the wagons in the rear and brought rations to us in the valley between Missionary Ridge and Lookout Mountain. For the first eight days these rations consisted of cornbread and bran coffee, but on the eighth day Ramy Lafitte, our company cook, got in possession of a yearling calf and made jerked beef of it. This was an addition to our bill of fare and we ate it with a good relish. At that time we were close to the enemy and some of our men would go near enough to talk with their outposts and sometimes trade with them giving tobacco in exchange for coffee. In this way we found out that they too were sometimes almost without provisions.

Rosecrans was relieved and Grant and Sherman came to take his place and with them came supplies and recruits, and it could be seen that active preparations were going on. We felt that woe would be to us if we did not get help pretty soon. Gen. Longstreet's corps was at Knoxville but slipped out and returned to Gen. Lee in Virginia.

There was always somebody to keep the Federals

fully informed as to our positions and numbers, and when Grant learned that Longstreet's corps had left, he commenced a forward movement. I was not in a position to know how he got his army across the Tennessee River. His first move was to take Lookout Mountain on our left front. We had been idle ever since the Battle of Chickamauga.

CHAPTER XXIV

MISSIONARY RIDGE BATTLE
GENERAL JOSEPH E. JOHNSTON RETURNS

On November 25th, our army abandoned the rifle pits in front of Missionary Ridge and retired to rifle pits on the summit of Missionary Ridge. The enemy's forces took Lookout Mountain easily enough and then advanced and crossed Chickamauga Creek. They advanced with opposition on Missionary Ridge to our left. Our men in rifle pits on the ridge were about one man every ten or fifteen feet, and we were attacked in front. We could not check the advance of the enemy because they were three lines deep and our men in single file in the trenches. We did some good shooting but there were not enough of us. When the Federals which were on the left of us in the ridge were coming from that direction, making an enfilading fire on us, it was either leave the trenches or be killed, so we left them. We didn't leave soon enough because we lost many of our best men before we got out of the range of their guns. Our loved Col. Winans was killed on this ridge. This was in the evening. We retired about four miles and bivouacked for the night.

The next day the army marched to Dalton, Georgia. Here another change in commanders took place. Gen. Joseph E. Johnston, the commander we had needed ever since he was relieved at Jackson, Mississippi was sent to us again with orders to take Bragg's army and drive the Federal army out of Georgia at once. Great was the rejoicing by the soldiers of this little army when Johnston came to our relief and Braxton Bragg was out. He took command of this depleted army and instead of obeying such an order and having his men slaughtered, acted on his own better judgement. First there must be quarters prepared for the fast approaching winter. Then provisions gathered for man and beast, and at the same time, watch every movement of the enemy and allow no surprises.

After the Battle of Missionary Ridge the Federal army was placed under the command of Gen. Sherman, the best general in the United States Army. Gen. Grant was sent to Virginia as commander-in-chief of all the Federal armies and took command personally of the armies which confronted Gen. R. E. Lee. On again assuming command of our army Gen. Johnston gave notice that he was with us and for victory over the enemy.

My first house at Dalton was made of cornstalks. I built the walls three feet high and long enough and wide enough to spread a blanket over a bed of straw on the inside. I secured a piece of tenting, or duck cloth, wide enough to stretch over my house, resting it on a little pole supported at each end by a fork of the same material as the pole. This turned the rain, and a little ditch on the sides outside of the house conveyed the falling water away from my bed. When the wagons came I had a good supply of warm blankets. My messmates were not with me now. Frank Smith, the captain of our company, was away on sick leave, and I have already written of the other one. I took charge of the roll of bedding and when it was spread out over the straw in my cornstalk house, there was a good place to sleep. But I was not allowed to enjoy it alone. The weather was cold, and Joe Williams and Con Conway had lost their blankets in the Battle of Missionary Ridge and had not been fortunate enough to secure any more. They were members of my company and were from Keachie, Louisiana. I took them into my house. This made three of us to share this bed. We were warm and comfortable until we built a larger house. Houses large enough for four beds or eight men were built of poplar timber. The trees were large and easily split into slabs 4 x 6 inches and 14 feet long. Boards were made of poplar and other timbers to cover the houses and it was not long before our army was sheltered; and I may safely say, enjoying the cold winter. There were snow-ball battles, with charges and counter charges by brigades and divisions, accompanied with the familiar so called 'rebel yell,' as when grape and canister and minnie balls had been used instead of snowballs. Gen. Joseph E. Johnston was possessed of a magnetism which held such sway over his army that there was a feeling of security pervading every part of it. There was no fear of surprise nor defeat, and the soldiers passed the time while we were in Dalton in various ways. There were religious services, and able preachers in soldiers garb delivered sermons to appreciative listeners. There were debating clubs, games at cards, chess and checkers and very little drilling. There were baptisms in a clear running stream when these soldiers of the Confederate army became 'Soldiers of the Cross' and of the army which was battling against immorality and wickedness in its varied forms.

CHAPTER XXV

A FURLOUGH AND VISIT WITH COUSINS

Dalton was situated 100 miles north of Atlanta on the railroad and it was made so secure that Gen. Sherman was afraid to make an assault on the place after the winter was gone and the spring days reminded the generals that activities must begin. Some soldiers received furloughs during February, 1864, for a few days. Wesley Powell, a member of our company, drew one for seven days. By consent of the Captain I bought it from him. He said he could not go home across the Mississippi and sold it to me because I could use it to visit relatives in Alabama near our old camp ground at Pollard. It meant a recreation for me if I could succeed in getting there. I went to the depot and after much perseverance and long waiting, finally obtained transportation papers and got on the cars. The night was very cold and I was almost frozen when the train arrived at Atlanta a little before daylight. I went to an inn and procured a drink of good whiskey. I felt like it would at least make me warmer and it did. John Mc-Cormick, a member of our regiment, was with me, and on a like errand, was spending a few days away from the army. We went to a restaurant and called for one dozen eggs. We paid $9.00 for them. This was not because of depreciation in our money but because of the pure 'cussidness' of the dealer, added to the scarcity of eggs when the demand was so great.

At Opelika, Alabama while our train was waiting, a

young lady presented me with a basket of provisions and would not accept any money from me for it. There were several furloughed soldiers with me and she must have selected me as the most hungry looking 'Confed' in the crowd. We jointly shared the contents of the basket and when I gave it back to her she found a piece of leather in the bottom of it. Holding it up she said. "Take this too, you may need it." I accepted this basket of provisions with thanks in language the best I could command. Just then the train started and I waved my hat as long as I could see her. She responded with the wave of a white handkerchief which called to mind the cheering approvals of our Southern girls everywhere. It was not their fault that the Confederate States government was overthrown and destroyed.

I arrived at Evergreen in the evening of February 5th, 1864, and stopped that night in a hotel. The next morning I went out to an old Frenchman's house for breakfast. This was Mr. Desplooce who had visited our regiment frequently when we were camped at Pollard. I knew where he lived and I knew, too, that he would treat me royally and would want to hear from his other acquaintances of the Nineteenth Louisiana Infantry. After breakfast he took me in his buggy to visit my Aunt Elizabeth McPherson, whose widowed daughter, Mrs. Tomlinson, and grand daughters, Isadore and Augusta Tomlinson, were living with her. I spent two days with them and then went to cousin Lawrence Cater's house near Burnt Corn, where I met him and his estimable wife, cousin Fannie, and their only child Ned. We went on the Sabbath to her father's home, where we heard

one of his Negroes preach. The sermon was really
uplifting and edifying. At its conclusion he asked a
fellow servant, an old man, to pray. The prayer was so
earnest and feelingly offered it showed there was no
doubting in his faith as to the reality of the religion of
Jesus of Nazareth. With falling tears he asked God to
take care of his young master (then a prisoner in the
hands of the Federals) and prayed for his safe return
home. I thought of the misguided and misinformed
fanatical followers of Wm. Lloyd Garrison and Harriet
Beecher Stowe who had already deluged our country in
blood, and were only waiting while the cold weather
lasted, to renew the carnage when balmy spring days
came again. I spent a night and one half day with my
father's old friend and neighbor, John D. Cary, at Sparta. His sister, Miss Fannie, and his daughter Miss Kate,
sang, and played the piano. I had not forgotten all of
my pieces of piano music and when a violin was brought
into requisition, I contributed to our entertainment.
Mrs. Cary, knowing that but a day or two would pass
before my meals would be 'hard tack' corn dodgers,
poor beef and bran coffee, had her table supplied with
everything (it seemed to me) good to eat while I was
their guest. There, too, the family carriage with a span
of pretty bays, and the driver who would not swap places
with either Mr. Lincoln or Mr. Davis if such a swap were
offered, was at our service.

Sparta was where I 'first saw the light of day,' twenty-three years before, and I desired to see all of the old
town, which was now showing the result of neglect; and
with the courthouse already moved to Evergreen on the

railroad, the town was rapidly passing away. Misses
Fannie and Kate and I took seats inside the carriage,
and the driver, desiring to show the metal of the bays,
gave us a rapid ride to the different parts of the town
and out to New Sparta, a station on the railroad three
miles distant. When we returned, dinner was an-
nounced as ready. A fat gobbler, roasted to suit the
most fastidious epicurean, awaited the carving knife.
After dinner I had to say good-bye to these dear friends.
My furlough was too limited to allow a longer enjoy-
ment of the pleasures of Mr. Cary's house. I had
promised cousin Lawrence, on leaving, to visit his sister
Kate at Montgomery, before I took the train for Dalton.
She was a playmate in our childhood the year my
father's family were in Harrison County, Texas. She,
with her two little daughters, Bella and Tennie, were
boarding with her aunt, Mrs. Powell, in Montgomery,
while her husband Charley McVoy was in the army. She,
too, was sad when I left the next morning enroute for
Dalton.

When I arrived at Dalton I found myself a leader of
a brass band which had been organized in the regiment
during my absence. We (I mean the members of the
brass band) now sadly missed Col. Winans who, as
before stated, was killed at the Battle of Missionary
Ridge. Lieut. Col. R. W. Turner was now the colonel of
the regiment. He didn't care very much for music, but
gave permission for the organization of the brass band.
Col. Winans loved music and would have helped me
and would have taken much interest in our success.
Before the Battle of Chickamauga Gen. Dan Adams

had asked Col. Winans to let him have me for his brigade bugler. He told Winans that he had not been able to get a man that would stay with him in battle. Col. Winans told him that I would stay with him, but said he would not order me to go but would leave the decision with me. Adams said he would furnish a horse and saddle and would take me in his mess with him. I said, "Col. Winans, I am like Ruth to Naomi, I am staying with you." And that settled the matter.

I worked faithfully with my band. We were excused from all other duty for the time, but there were no musicians among my men and this made the task really hard. They were determined not to relax their efforts to learn, and we spent the balance of the time we were at Dalton, in practice with those 'brass horns.' There was one man in the band who could not gain any proficiency with his part, but he had done more and worked harder in 'getting up' this band, buying the instruments, etc., and tried more faithfully to learn than all the others, and I was determined to keep him at 'all hazards.' I gave him the 3rd alto, the easiest part. The others called him "Professor," and this name he carried as long as we had an army. I arranged the music as simple and easy as possible. On the 20th of March we played our first tattoo for the regiment. After that we played for roll call and dress parade.

CHAPTER XXVI

SPRINGTIME – WAR RENEWAL
DESERTERS SHOT

Spring was bringing warmer days and Gen. Johnston issued an order that the soldiers must get rid of their long hair and beards, and there were some busy days in camp with scissors and razors. Of course, this made a changed appearance among the 'boys' and our regiment, when on parade or review with their brass band, manifested a pride in the change. The camp of the Louisianians and Texans was now their home. The Mississippi River was infested with Federals; and their gunboats, from its mouth to Mason's and Dixon's line since the fall of Vicksburg, were between them and the homes they had left to repel the invaders.

It is imperative that man should adjust himself to his environments and so at Dalton, with the watchful Johnston as chief, time had passed almost unnoticed by his army. A mail carrier appears upon the scene and an opportunity comes for receiving and answering letters from friends and from home. Mr. Braden, a member of the Nineteenth La. Infantry, who was the man I had helped to carry on a stretcher to a distant field hospital at the Battle of Chickamauga, had gotten well but was permanently too disabled to carry a musket, so he was the mail carrier. He had found a place somewhere on the Mississippi River where he could be carried in a skiff across the river, and return. The General had given him a passport so that he would not be hindered by any authorities on his route. He brought letters to the regiment, and I received one from home and one from Cousin Em. Some letters were from the friends in Alabama whom I had visited when on my bought furlough. I answered these letters during my rest spells from band practice. It did not require postage stamps to send my letters, but it did require that 'soldier letters' have the name of command written somewhere on the envelope. The person addressed had to pay ten cents to get possession of the letter. This was the law but I am sure my letters were not worth that much money. And then too, ten cents had to be prepaid on letters coming to the soldiers.

Picket firing in front, May 2d, reminded us that the Federals had decided to dispossess us of our winter quarters. Well, we could do without them, if necessary, but we were not yet ready to leave them. The army took position in the breast works but the enemy retired and our soldiers returned in the evening. I attended a prayer meeting at night. Our soldiers loved those religious exercises at Dalton. Don't think, dear reader, that you will find cowards among Godfearing men when duty calls them.

It is May 4th. I witnessed and took part in a sad scene. While the enemy is in front and preparing to advance, Gen. Johnston is called upon to pass the death sentence on two men who had deserted. Painful and heart rending the duty, but such is the military law. The leader of the band of the Twentieth La. Regiment of our brigade, requested me to take the place of his cornet player who was sick, in playing the "Dead March" as we marched around the square formed by a brigade of armed soldiers. The condemned men had been blindfolded and sat on their coffins on one side of the square. Twelve men had been detailed and were furnished twelve muskets, half of which were loaded with blank cartridges and the other half with full loaded buck and ball cartridges. None of the twelve men knew who had drawn muskets with blank cartridges, but all were ordered to aim at the breasts of the condemned men; when the word was given they had taken position ten paces in front of the blindfolded men and were ordered to "make ready, aim, fire." I turned my face in another direction as the order was given and when I again looked at the condemned men they were prostrate across their coffins. Death had come to them with the report of the muskets.

The next day, May 5th, our division took position in the breastworks but our cavalry repulsed the enemy confronting us, and we returned to our quarters in the evening. This was to be our last night at Dalton. Our wagons were sent south to Resaca on the railroad. Information came to us that General Sherman had 100,000 men. Of these, McPherson had 25,000 on our left, Thomas had 60,000 on our front, Schofield had 15,000 on our right, and 250 cannons. Of course our little army could not meet these successfully in open combat. Only Joseph E. Johnston could cope with this situation. I was not so situated as to know of many things that transpired, but I did know of the faith our soldiers had in their commander, and they feared no surprise nor wrong movement. When a retrograde was ordered they knew it was to get a better position to meet Sherman's overwhelming numbers. All of his attacks at Dalton were repulsed, and he attempted to get a part of his army in our rear at Resaca. There was much heavy cannonading in Snake Creek Gap, but the charge made by the enemy was repulsed. The fighting near Resaca was continued several days. Gen. Hood was to make an attack on the 15th. The General had lost a leg at Chickamauga and was slower in obeying orders than when he commanded his brigade in Gen. Lee's army. At any rate, he failed to make the attack promptly, but later in the day placed a battery of four cannons on a high position. These the enemy took, also his hospitals, but General Wheeler, with two brigades, retook them on the same day, captured forty prisoners, and drove the enemy two miles. General Wheeler's cavalry was worth more to us now than can be estimated. Sherman's army crossed the Oristenola River that night and this caused the evacuation of Resaca.

My band was put in the infirmary corps and I was ordered to go to the wagons and take care of the band instruments. The wagons were at Kingston. I marched about eighteen miles but night overtook me and I slept on the roadside under a large tree. The heavy foliage of this tree protected me from the falling dew. The armies on both sides were now very active, with Sherman continuing his efforts to get in our rear. Our wagons had to be kept in the rear but not far away because our cooks had to carry provisions to the soldiers in front.

CHAPTER XXVII

RETREAT FROM DALTON — CHANGE OF COMMANDERS — DISASTER FOLLOWS

The next heavy fighting was at Kenesaw Mountain. All of Sherman's attacks were repulsed, but he continued his efforts to get in our rear. These moves caused almost continuous engagements. The cooks brought a report which I repeat here: "The dry grass and undergrowth had been set on fire by the artillery during the Battle at Kenesaw Mountain in front of Pat Cleburne's division and the enemy's wounded were in danger of being burned to death. Cleburne's men saw this and called to the enemy to come and get their wounded comrades before the fire got to them. By common consent a truce was effected for that purpose and our soldiers assisted in taking their wounded enemies out of danger of the burning grass and weeds. After the time was declared ended our men returned to their line of battle and the enemy did the same."

Sherman continued to try to force Johnston into a battle at a disadvantage. He would take a position and build breastworks and then invite an attack by throwing forward his skirmishers, but Gen. Johnston knew the strength of his opponent and would not allow his men to attack Sherman's breastworks. He seemed to know every design of Sherman, who to bring on an engagement, had to fight our army in breastworks, resulting always in heavy losses to his army. This battling and retreating continued until we were near Atlanta. Captain N. G. Pearson of Mansfield, Louisiana, was killed near Marietta on the 28th. My friendship with him dated from my boyhood. He was captain of a company in our regiment; a brave and good man. A few days afterwards Bishop Polk, an able General and Christian soldier, was killed on Pine Mountain by a cannon ball, while examining in company with Gen. Johnston, an exposed position occupied by Gen. Bate's division. This, too, was a sad loss to our army. Men in the varied walks of life in time of peace, now soldiers in defense of their country, were offering up their lives daily in this invasion.

At times the determination of the enemy to take our rifle pits in the series of battles on our retreat from Dalton to Atlanta, moved them to acts of daring worthy of a better cause. On one occasion some of our men were bayonetted in the rifle pits before an onslaught could be checked, but it resulted in terrible destruction of the Federals, as they were forced to fall back. A truce was agreed to, to permit the enemy to bury their dead.

I was with the wagons in the rear sometimes, and at other times I would be alone. I slept one night on the plowed ground in a field under a peach tree near Cartersville. When I overtook the wagons the next evening, I was hungry as well as tired, and I remained with them that night. I met some of my old comrades of the Third Texas. The regiment was mounted now and doing hard service with Gen. Wheeler. They were enroute to intercept some Federal cavalry who were reconnoitering to find the best way for Sherman's army.

Leaving the wagons the next day, I got on the cars and went to Atlanta.

There I met my old messmate and friend, First Lieutenant A. C. Rorrison of Company B, Third Texas Cavalry, and was with him two days in the city. It took us some time to tell of our adventures since we separated at Tupelo, Mississippi in August, 1862. We spoke of the continued fighting all the way from Dalton, and as our commands were not yet at Atlanta, much had to be done before they arrived there, and it was not easy to foretell results. He said Sherman was obeying orders, and if Johnston was not hindered by interference from President Davis and continued his present mode of warfare, Sherman and his whole army would be prisoners in our hands before the summer was over. He said also that if Gen. Pemberton had evacuated Vicksburg and had taken his army across Big Black River to Gen. Johnston when first ordered to do so, the Mississippi River would not have been closed to the Confederacy. I told him that since I had been ordered to take charge of my band instruments and remain with the wagons, I had talked with people who were ignorant of the strength of the two armies and were making serious complaints about their country being overrun by these armies of soldiers. They believed Gen. Johnston was at fault for not driving Sherman out of Georgia. I told him also that I had told these people that if the Georgia people succeeded in getting rid of Johnston, that Sherman would make an ash heap of the whole state. Lieut. Rorrison said, "Old Jeff is too smart a man to allow things like that to influence him. We hear that personally he does not like him but he certainly ought to have confidence in his generalship. We all know that Joseph E. Johnston is by far the best general in the Confederate army." Lieut. Rorrison and I attended church together on Sunday as we had done in Henderson, Texas and we heard a good sermon from the text, "Mary hath chosen that better part." We got news in the evening that Generals Cheatham's and Cleburne's divisions had been attacked but had repulsed and inflicted a heavy loss on the enemy. We then separated. He returned to his regiment and I returned to our wagons which were then at Fayetteville. Sherman crossed the Chattahoochee River and dug entrenchments, expecting an attack. Our army crossed the same river and was entrenched between Sherman and Atlanta.

I received very sad news from the regiment at the front in the evening. They had listened to shouts from the entire line of Sherman's army and feared that they had received news of another victory by the Federals in Virginia, but it was news of far greater importance to them. They had received news that Gen. Johnston had been removed and that Gen. John B. Hood was in command of the Confederate army. They knew what would follow. There would be no more charging of Confederate rifle pits, no more hindrance to getting in the rear of the Confederate army, but there would be a necessity to build breastworks in which to receive and repel the charges of Hood's army.

Here is Gen. Joseph E. Johnston's reward for shielding his soldiers and inflicting losses in Gen. Sherman's army until his own little army could successfully offer battle and turn back the advancing hosts of Sherman's invaders. "July 17, 1864. Lieutenant General John B. Hood has been commissioned to the temporary rank of General under the late law of Congress and you are informed that as you have failed to arrest the advance of the enemy in the vicinity of Atlanta, far in the interior of Georgia, and express no confidence that you can defeat or repel him, you are hereby relieved from the command of the army and Department of Tennessee, which you will immediately turn over to Gen. Hood."

This order sounded the death knell to the government of the Confederate States of America. The mistake that our soldiers then made was in not laying down their arms and stopping further bloodshed. They knew that Braxton Bragg, a personal friend of the chief executive, had something to do with this order from Richmond, Virginia. The order was read to the army and obeyed fully. Another order was read to our army. "In obedience to orders of the War Department, I turn over to General Hood the command of the army and Department of Tennessee. I cannot leave this noble army without expressing my admiration of the high military qualities it has displayed. A long and arduous campaign has made conspicuous every soldierly virtue, endurance to toil, obedience to orders, brilliant courage. The enemy has never attacked but to be repulsed and severely punished. You soldiers have never argued but from your courage, and never counted your foes. No longer your leader, I will still watch your career and will rejoice in your victories. To one and all

I offer assurance of my friendship and bid you an affectionate farewell. Joseph E. Johnston, General." After hearing Gen. Johnston's farewell letter read, of course our hearts were filled with sadness. We loved him, we were proud to be commanded by so great and gifted a soldier. He knew nothing of fear, but felt deeply the great responsibility which was upon him because of the perfect confidence in him of all his soldiers, and he shielded them against unnecessary exposures of life. He always knew when and where to use them in defeating the plans of the great General who was endeavoring to crush him with an army of determined soldiers doubly outnumbering his own at Dalton, but not at Atlanta. Gen. Sherman when informed of the change in commanders of our army, made preparations to act on the defense and placed his men behind breastworks. Someone of his army has since written and made public this statement, "Just at this time (meaning after the armies had crossed the Chattahoochee River), much to our comfort and to his surprise, Johnston was removed and Hood placed in command of the Confederate army. Johnston had planned to attack Sherman at Peachtree Creek, expecting just such a division between our wings as we made."

This change of commanders when we were in line of battle had an effect on the army that was hard to overcome. Our president had lost his exalted place in our esteem. He was a statesman with a splendid record and for this we honored him. As commander-in-chief of all the armies he was a failure, with no control over his personal dislikes for those who differed from his opinions. But the people of the state of Georgia had prayed to him for help and to give them a general who could and would drive Sherman's army out of Georgia. And then there was Braxton Bragg, whose magnetism over Davis was wonderful, forgetting no doubt, that Sherman had toyed with him at Chattanooga like a cat playing with a crippled mouse. He appeared upon the scene and used his influence against our General Johnston, and recommended Hood as a 'mighty warrior' who could and would put Sherman back across the Tennessee River in double quick time. And so our president yielded and the change was made. It was for us to forgive him and do our duty. Our judgement would not let us admit that there was any hope for us now.

The end could not be very far away. So different from that of the Revolution when the thirteen colonies threw off the yoke of Great Britain. There was no ocean of bounding billows to separate us. Different because 'twas fearful to think of the many precious lives to be blotted out before that end came. Johnston's motto "Never sacrifice men for position" would never be remembered now. Hood visited Johnston but not to insist as was afterwards said, that he remain in command until after the expected battle, but to ascertain his plans. Gen. Johnston gave them to him with some suggestions as to how to make the attack, but these were ignored entirely. He fell upon the entrenched hosts of Sherman at once, only to be repulsed with fearful slaughter. This brought a visit to our part of the army from General S. D. Lee. He made us a speech. Among other things he said, "Soldiers, you can take temporary breastworks, you must and you shall take temporary breastworks." This was what he felt about it, but he was not in the charge on foot with a musket when our men were forced back, and it seemed to me that he might have had better success with his speech if he had used different language. I was near him when he spoke and it made me feel like he had lost respect for us. He certainly had no more at stake than the rest of us. I was sorry he said it.

A retreat from the position was the only remedy. Our commander had not exercised any good judgement and this attack was only a foretaste of what was ahead of us. I received a special order from Col. Turner of our regiment, to leave my band instruments in the care of our wagon driver and to report at once with a musket to members of my regiment and answer to roll call in my company. His order was promptly obeyed. The members of my band were already in the infirmary corps.

My first duty was to go to the ordnance wagon and bring ammunition to the regiment. I had to go to and from the wagon across a skirt of timber where there was an artillery duel. Arthur Newman, our ordnance sergeant, said on seeing me, "Hello, I thought you were with the baggage wagons." I told him I had been, but Col. Turner notified me that I was needed in the regiment, and I am here. Arthur knew about where the regiment was and asked me how I managed to get to him across that skirt of timbered woods under that artillery fire. I told him they shot above me, and I must hurry back before the infantry charged. I got back safely with the cartridges but heard several minnie balls whistle past me. The sharpshooters had commenced to fall back.

This preceded an attack in which we lost one officer and fifteen privates killed, sixteen officers and eighty-two privates wounded, and ten missing or prisoners. The enemy captured 121 of our brigade on picket, but we established our line.

After several days of attack, fruitless of course, and with heavy losses, Gen. Hood decided to occupy the breastworks around Atlanta which Gen. Johnston had built there, but he was too late. Sherman had gained too great an advantage by this time to attack breastworks. He didn't have to do this. The weather was hot, but we had to stay in ditches. Our clothes were soon the color of the clay in which we were protected from shells and minnie balls. We could not leave the ditches in the daytime without danger of being killed at any moment. The different regiments were sometimes relieved, and marched at night in rear of the breastworks beyond range of the enemy's missiles, where we rested for twenty-four hours, after which we again took our places in the breastworks. We had confidence in Generals Hardee, Cheatham, Stewart, Cleburne, and S. D. Lee (not-with-standing his harsh language in the speech referred to some days back) and hoped they would have some influence for good with our brave and daring commander in this ordeal through which we were passing.

After several days we were taken out of the

breastworks at Atlanta and marched away from the city, now occupied by the Federals. I was detailed to go on picket duty. I was one of three men of the picket line left at a place with a pick to dig a redoubt or hole to protect us from the enemy's sharpshooters. This was in a ravine in an open field near a timbered forest in which the enemy had a line of sharpshooters. They saw us when we were left there by the lieutenant who commanded us. There was an old dead tree about fifteen inches or more in diameter, some ten paces from us. When we commenced to dig our redoubt, we were fired on by a single picket from the enemy in that forest but none of us were struck. We saw the smoke of the gun of the Federal and we got behind the dead tree opposite from where we saw the smoke of that gun; one man against the tree, a second man behind him and the third after the second. This seemed to be fun for the Federal who took a second shot at us. He was a good marksman, the ball from his gun struck the tree. We did not move for that, but he shot again and this time the ball came through the side of the tree and struck one of our men in the arm. He, of course, had to leave to get his arm dressed. There were some large rocks in a little dry branch just in rear of us and my companion and I crawled to those rocks and we each got a rock and lay behind it as flat as a fox squirrel when hiding from a hunter. We pushed the rocks in front of us to where we had commenced digging our redoubt. That Fed was having a picnic all by himself. He was not over seventy-five yards from us and continued to shoot while we were digging.

We made slow progress with our pick because we were prostrate on the ground behind our rocks. My rock was struck once before I got it to where I wanted it, and once while digging behind it. We thought it safer not to return the fire until we could get into our redoubt. We finished it after so long a time and took a shot each at the place where we saw the smoke from the Fed's rifle. He did not reply to our fire. He could see us but we could not see him and we supposed he had become a little careless because of our not returning his fire and allowed himself to be exposed. When he did not reply, our conclusion was that he had either decided 'discretion was the better part of valor' or was to be numbered with those in Sherman's cemetery at Marietta. We had commenced to feel pretty safe in our redoubt when we were moved to another place and spent the balance of that day and night in digging redoubts and ditching. We were relieved the next morning. I was tired and sleepy.

Something had 'come over the spirit of Colonel Turner's dreams' or else a new plan of action had been mapped out by General Hood. On returning to the regiment from picket duty Col. Turner ordered me to go to the wagons and take charge of the band instruments and the baggage of the regiment.

My experiences in the army were varied. I went in a crowded box car to Griffin and slept that night under a car shed. When morning came I found the wagons and ate breakfast with the teamsters. Finding the band instruments and the baggage all right, I visited our wounded in a hospital in Griffin. Of course they were suffering from their wounds but were receiving good attention. The ladies were giving necessary assistance and their presence and words of cheer were worth more to suffering soldiers than I have words to express. One of our wounded told me that Gen. M. D. Ector was in a private house nearby and badly wounded. I have already told who he was, and I went to see him. His daughter, Miss Jennie, had found her way to him and he certainly needed her. One of his legs had been shot away by a cannonball. He was recovering as fast as could be expected and was cheerful. He asked me to send his love to Cousin Em Reagan if I got a chance to send a letter across the Mississippi River, and to say to her that his navigation had been impeded and he would be away from his brigade for a time. He hoped to get well and be with the 'boys' at the front again soon. After visiting Gen. Ector, I went to Forsyth and found some of the wounded of our regiment at a hospital there. Capt. Smith of our company, was on the sick list and had not been with his company for a year. He was at his grandfather's, not far from Forsyth, and I went out to see him. He was still unfit for duty in camp. I returned to Griffin and to the wagons.

The Federals had evacuated their breastworks in Atlanta on the 27th, and on the 30th were reported massing on our left. Our division moved below East Point, and on the 31st, moved near Jonesborough. Hardee's and Lee's corps attacked the enemy on that date. Hardee's corps carried the enemy's breastworks but Lee's corps were repulsed. Lieutenant Powell of our company was captured. Our regiment lost 48 men and our brigade 200 men. This was in killed, wounded, and missing. Our army evacuated Atlanta on September 1st. Hardee's Corps attacked the enemy on the 1st and 2d, but gained nothing except protecting our retreat to Jonesborough where we went into camp near Lovejoy Station. Here the members of my band were permitted to leave the infirmary corps and report to me for duty. My cornet player had been killed and another member was wounded and in the hospital, but there were two members of the Fourth La. band left. Joe Moore and Theodore Bauer were permitted to come into my band. There was work for me now. After practicing or rehearsing some pieces, for a change, we serenaded a family of good people in the vicinity, who appreciated it and gave us a nice treat. We were at Lovejoy several days. A letter came to me here, from home. Sister Vic wrote to me that my little brother Junius, who was nine years old, had died. This was the third brother I had lost since I was at home in January 1861. I also received a letter from Cousin Em from her home in Rusk County, Texas. She was not as cheerful as formerly. She had heard of our change in commanders, but had not heard of the slaughter at Atlanta, nor of our defeat.

CHAPTER XXVIII

MORE MARCHING — SHOE PROBLEMS

On the 17th we commenced a march toward Fayetteville and camped near the M. & A. Railroad. On the 18th we continued our march and camped near Fayetteville. On the 19th we marched twenty-two miles and bivouacked near Palmetto. On the twentieth we marched four miles, formed in line of battle and commenced building breastworks, for what purpose I never knew. It began to dawn on us now, that Sherman would have nothing more to fear from our army, and that the state of Georgia was at his mercy. One the 21st we changed from our position to one on the right of the battle line and spent the day at work on fortifications. I was not situated so that I could get information as to the cause of our strange move. I could not believe that we would be attacked at that place. It was evident that Sherman was not paying any attention to Gen. Hood's movements. Lieut. Powell had been exchanged and returned to his company. He said from what he could learn, it was surmised that we had started for Nashville, Tennessee, and that Sherman, on account of this would change his southeast march and try to intercept Hood somewhere about the Tennessee River. I did not believe any of these surmises. There were plenty of Federal soldiers in Tennessee to look after Hood while Sherman could destroy Georgia and take his army to Gen. Grant in front of Lee in Virginia.

We were at Palmetto several days. On the 29th we

marched till ten o'clock at night, then rested until daylight on the 30th, and crossed the Chattahoochee River at sunrise, eight miles from Palmetto. It was intimated that we were making a flank movement expecting to attack the enemy where he was not looking for us. This was all nonsense. Sherman was not paying any attention to Hood now. He didn't have to. We marched seventeen miles in the rain and mud, then camped. There were heavy rains; no enemy in sight. We continued our march on October 2d and 3d and halted about noon near Lost Mountain. We listened to cannonading in the direction of Marietta and commenced digging rifle pits. We were at that place on the 4th and 5th. The rains were heavy every day and night, though not continuous. We marched in rain and mud to Dallas on the 6th and bivouacked there at night. On the 7th we marched over a mountainous region and camped near Van Wort. On the 8th we continued our march. The morning was cold with wind from the north. We camped two miles from Cedar Town. On the 9th it seemed that Hood was expecting trouble. My band was again put on the infirmary corps, and Joe Moore and I were left with the baggage wagons to take care of the band instruments. The wagons crossed Big Cedar River and parked. On the 10th they passed through Cave Springs and crossed the state line into Alabama and parked in Cherokee County. We parked on the 12th near Coosa River, passed through Santro on Jacksonville Road; on the 14th passed through Jacksonville and parked near the town on the 15th. We left Jacksonville on the 20th in the afternoon and traveled seven miles. I left the wagons after we crossed Coosa River at Gadsden on the 21st. Col. Turner had changed again. He seemed to think that, as matters stood now, there was no necessity for a regimental band and ordered me to come back to my company with a musket. We marched four miles.

I was with the army now. We bivouacked on Sand Mountain on the 23d, crossed Warren River on the 24th, marched on the 25th and 26th and passed through Summerville - all under heavy rains and on muddy roads. I could hardly navigate on account of the mud and hunger and no rations. I write not only of myself but also of Hood's army. It was true that we had started for Nashville. For what purpose I could not tell. Sherman could easily send troops by railroad to Nashville to repeat the Atlanta tragedy. But he was not needed. Gen. Thomas had men enough without calling on Sherman to drive us out of Tennessee. Perhaps I should not write about these unfortunate conditions but should tell only of my individual experiences as a Confederate soldier. I have already said that there was no silver lining to the cloud overhanging us. Our God was not favoring our enemies, but they had sense enough to profit by our childish errors. On the 27th of October we marched eighteen miles on heavy roads; 28th, eighteen miles and bivouacked on M. & C. Railroad near Courtland; 19th, marched some eighteen miles passing through Courtland and Cleveland; 30th, I was sick with severe cold and fever. I asked Dr. Philson, our regimental surgeon, to advise me what to do, as I was about to 'fall by the wayside.' He said he didn't know

what to say to me, but if possible to stay with the
regiment. My shoes had worn out and for two days I
had been wearing a pair of moccasins made of cowskin
freshly taken off a poor beef. They had not worn out
but had separated into many parts from being in soft
mud so long. A soldier brought me a pair of shoes
number four size and said I could have them for four
dollars. I bought them without asking any questions. I
believed he had stolen them because no such shoes had
been issued to the soldiers. A number six was as small
a shoe as I could wear, but by cutting away enough of
the vamp to free my toes, I could wear them. They were
quite an improvement over my moccasins. Dr. Philson
told me my change in footwear would enable me to stay
with the regiment, and that if I did not get discouraged
I would soon be well. This proved true.

Our brigade crossed the Tennessee River on a pontoon bridge and took the town of Florence. It was
occupied by a small garrison of Federals. One man was
killed. The others retreated towards Columbia. We
were in camp a week at Florence. The people were glad
we had come. They had been under Federal rule for
some time but here I heard of no cases of ill treatment
by the Federal soldiers.

We moved out two miles from the town and camped
until the 20th of November. While there, I received
some letters from home and from relatives in Alabama
and had an opportunity to send one home. We left on
the 20th and continued our march on the 21st and
continued for three more days through poor country.
The weather was cold with snow and the roads were

heavy. We passed through Henryville on the 24th. On the 25th we passed through Mt. Pleasant in beautiful country. The next day we passed the beautiful residences of Generals Pillow and Polk in a fertile, and I believe, as pretty a country as I ever saw. Walnut groves, fine residences and good farms gave evidence of a prosperous people, their country not yet destroyed by the ravages of a pillaging soldiery.

Orders were very strict in our command that any depredations or hog stealing would bring swift and severe punishment to the soldiers found guilty. We fared better in the Tennessee Valley on the Alabama side of the river, not in issued rations but by reason of good 'foraging' after nightfall. Particular attention was paid to the farms that were passed in the evening and to the ungathered crops. After going into camp at night, some members of our mess would go back to a field where there were ungathered crops and return with something to be cooked. If it was a pumpkin the night would be nearly gone before it could be thoroughly cooked. The man who had made the trip would be allowed to sleep but the others would watch the cooking by reliefs, so that all could get some sleep. A camp kettle (made of sheet iron), not very heavy and carried by turns on the march, had been called into requisition and served a good purpose; but up here in this rich country in Tennessee there were many fat hogs running at large in the field and where orders were so strict, the soldiers had to be very cautious. Sometimes we did not have enough corn to parch to satisfy hunger. One evening, one of our men, and by the way, this was my

3rd alto player when my band was in 'full swing,' came
to me and said, "I want your gun tomorrow morning.
When you wake up and find mine in the place of it, just
keep your own counsel, we've got to have some meat."
The weather was fearfully bad: rain, hail, ice and snow.
We needed something besides the rations we were
drawing.

I had fresh pork for breakfast. About an hour later
after I had eaten breakfast my man brought my gun and
got his own. He said, "Your gun saved me; there were
a dozen of us in line and a Lieutenant passed in front
of us, taking the gun of each man. When he inserted
his forefinger in the muzzle of it, he made a note in a
little book of the names of the men whose guns had
been shot (which left powder print on his finger), and
handed it back to the owner. He examined your gun
very closely because it was bright inside and out and he
said to me, 'You keep a nice gun, sir.'"

I said, "Professor, I thank you for the nice pork we
had for breakfast, but you must be sure to rub your gun
a little and get the powder out of the muzzle. If that
Lieutenant is a gentleman we will not hear any more
about those missing hogs. We all know that the
Federals will get all the hogs we leave."

He asked, "Hey man, you are not whipped are you?"

"No," I answered, "but it grieves me to have to feel
that so many splendid men are going to be sacrificed on
this trip to Nashville which we cannot hold even if we
take it."

He said, "General Forrest is here now and we sleep
soundly when we know that he is between us and the

enemy. When we take Nashville we can go back on the railroad to Atlanta and look after Sherman and his army, which we left to destroy Georgia while we are on this trip to Nashville."

I replied, "I am so glad to see you so hopeful; we will do the best we can, as there is much fighting ahead."

CHAPTER XXIX

HOOD ATTACKS — TERRIBLE SLAUGHTER

We camped about three miles from Columbia and did some skirmishing with the enemy. We (our part of the army) had flanked them and we were lying close enough to the Nashville road to see them as they passed by at night, but there was no order for action of any kind and they were not interrupted.

Our army crossed Duck River on pontoon bridges on the 30th of November. We passed Spring Hill and were halted near Franklin. General Hood had ordered Gen. Cheatham to make an attack on Spring Hill but Cheatham never received the order and, of course, there was no attack. He had wanted to make an attack at Spring Hill, but would not do so without orders from Hood. The enemy held a strong position at Franklin behind breastworks when Hood's army came up. Gen. Forrest went to Gen. Hood and informed him of the strong position held by the Federals and suggested that it would be safer to leave them there and endeavor, by a flank movement, to get between them and Nashville.

We are now going to witness a manifestation of General John B. Hood's great generalship. Does he order his whole army forward? Oh, no! There is a little field in front of the enemy's breastworks large enough for a little division to form a line across it. The army is halted; a division is sent across the field to take the enemy's breastworks. It failed and must retreat across that field under fire, the same as when facing the enemy. A second division makes the same effort and meets the same results. A third division, and another were sent, both with the same results. Gen. Cleburne and his staff and all their horses are left on the breastworks.

Our division is to make the next assault, but darkness has come and we must wait 'till the next morning. When the morning came we started. We must be careful lest we step on a dead or wounded soldier. We went across the same field to the breastworks. We met no opposition. The enemy had gone to Nashville. We found the trenches filled—not half filled—but filled with dead men, both Federals and Confederates. General Hood did not lose all his men; darkness had come to the relief of some of them, and these must now go on to Nashville. On December 1st we marched to the suburbs of that city. The battle at Franklin and the manner in which it was managed had not given us any encouragement.

Our division was on the south side of Nashville and our duty there was to build breastworks. But we could not work all the time at this, so we had to dig down in the earth to get out of the cold wind. We made holes to build fires in, and these holes had to be wide enough and long enough to spread our blankets and lie down at night. It rained and sleeted and rained again forming a crust of ice on the ground which made it difficult for our wagons or artillery or cavalry to move for ten days. There were no recruits for us, but it gave time for the Federal general to get all the recruits he needed to put

Hood and his little squad back across the Tennessee River. On the 10th, lager beer was added to our rations. This was appreciated on account of the cold weather.

On the 15th, our lines on the left were attacked. My old friend M. D. Ector's brigade was the first to face Federal cavalry, which was too strong in numbers to be turned back, and this little brigade had to retreat to a safer place. The next was Stovall's brigade and Bate's division which shared the same fate. This caused our army to fall back four miles, form a line and make breastworks. Our brigade was behind a rock fence, which made us feel pretty safe, but we worked all night to make it stronger.

The Federals renewed the attack along our entire front the next morning, December 16th. The battle raged with fearful destruction to both armies until about 4:00 o'clock in the afternoon when the enemy made a successful charge just to our left and carried the temporary breastworks of Stovall's brigade of Bate's division, which retreated in disorder. This caused some confusion and the main army began a retrograde movement. Gen. Forrest's cavalry did some good work now.

The enemy's cavalry were annoying us at every point, and it took skillful management to hold them in check. Gen. Chalmer's division of Forrest's cavalry held them back until after dark, allowing our main army to retreat in order.

The battle continued on the 17th, the enemy's cavalry charging our line, which had been formed to protect our retreat. Our brigade lost two regiments; the Fourth and Thirtieth La. Infantries were captured. Gen. S. D.

Lee distinguished himself by superb management in the two days at Nashville, and on the 17th; not only by reckless daring and exposure, which the fighting at close quarters made necessary, but by the ability with which he handled the men under his command in protecting our retreat. Gen. Gibson, of whom we were always proud, was not to blame for the capture of the Fourth and Thirtieth La. regiments of our brigade. The enemy's cavalry had gotten in our rear and the capture was unavoidable. This fight was continued until after nightfall. Gen. Lee was wounded in the evening and was succeeded by Major General Stevenson, General Chalmers, General Buford and General Tucker of Forrest's command. Our own Gen. S. D. Lee must have the credit for preventing a rout and perhaps the capture of our army. Tucker was captured in a skirmish after dark.

Our retreat continued on the 18th. The next day we crossed Duck River near Columbia. On the 20th we marched twenty-three miles in a cold rain. On the 21st we passed through Pulaski, and continued our march on the 22nd and 23d, through snow and very cold weather. We marched twenty miles on the 24th. On Christmas Day, I waded Shoal Creek, which seemed to me 100 yards wide and the water very swift. To prevent being washed downstream, I had to secure a pole to brace myself. I removed my clothes except my shoes. I had to keep them on to protect my feet from the rough cutting rocks on the bottom of the creek. I fastened my clothes on the end of my gun and held them above the water. I suffered from the extreme cold of both wind and water, but after getting across I put my clothes on and kindled a fire and was soon warm. The main army did not cross where our regiment crossed Shoal Creek. Bridges were built at other places for crossing. The army camped at the Tennessee River. Two gunboats came in sight but a few shots from our batteries turned them back. We crossed the river on the 27th on pontoon bridges and camped at night on the Memphis and Charleston Railroad near Florence. We continued our retreat unmolested on the 28th and 29th and camped near Bear Creek. On the 30th we continued our retreat. There was rain, sleet and snow at night. On the 31st, the last of the long to be remembered year of 1864, we continued our retreat, passing through Iuka and Burnsville.

January 1st, 1865, a beautiful Sabbath day, was not a day of rest for us. We marched 5-1/2 miles and camped. The next day we marched thirteen miles and bivouacked 3-1/2 miles from the Mobile and Ohio Railroad near Rienzi. We were leaving the Federals far in the rear but continued our heavy and tiresome marching. I was so tired at night I could hardly move. The Federals were paying no attention to us but were resting from their successful battles in Tennessee. Their cavalry may have been watching to see where we were trying to go. On the 5th we camped near Saltillo. On the 6th, we camped near Tupelo, our old drilling ground where, in the summer of 1862, we had a fine army; now nearly half of our soldiers were sick. It was there that I had joined brother Rufus, having been transferred from the Third Texas Cavalry.

CHAPTER XXX

GLOOM AND DESPAIR

How different now! A wrecked and shattered army with nothing but gloom before us. Comment is unnecessary. We remained at Tupelo until January 25th, when we marched to Okolona. We marched to Egypt on the 26th and to West Point on the 27th. These were stations on the railroad. We remained at West Point until February 1st. Here I lost sight of the army, except for our brigade, which was very small now. We got on the cars and were put off at Mobile, Alabama. The man who was on Van Dorn's staff at the Battle of Pea Ridge, Arkansas,(and to whom, after a hard ride to overtake the retreat, I had handed the note from a captain who had captured three barrels of whiskey and wanted to know from Van Dorn what to do with it) was now a major general and in command of the Department of Tennessee. This was Dabney Maury.

We went into camp in the suburbs of the city on February 3d for a little rest. Short furloughs were given some of our soldiers. I obtained one for a leave of six days and spent them with relatives and friends in Alabama, where I had spent a few days in February 1864. I spent a night at Evergreen and by private conveyance went to cousin Lawrence Cater's home near Burnt Corn. Cousin Fannie, his estimable wife, made me a nice present. It was a piece of Confederate jeans cloth. She went with me in a buggy to Belleville,

a nearby village, where Mrs. Finch, an expert
seamstress, took my measurements and cut out of that
cloth a Captain's style coat. Mrs. Finch made no charge
because I was a soldier. We returned in the evening to
cousin Fannie's home and I remained with them until
my coat was finished. When I put it on she said I had
too much long hair on my head to match that coat and
that she needed the hair for a pincushion. I consented
to the separation. I didn't know whether she could play
the barber or not, but when, with a pair of sharp scissors,
she had deprived me of my Samson looking locks and
put some finishing touches on my beard, she told me to
look in the glass, a large mirror which showed my entire
uniform. I did so, and told her I would just have to guess
it was I, as I could not see any resemblance to the hard
looking case who had arrived a day or two earlier!

This was my last visit with this loved family. Dear as
they had become to me, I had to leave them, and
forever. Cousin Lawrence carried me in his buggy to
the nearest railroad station. I left that train at
Lethatchie Station and walked out in the country
several miles to the residence of Mr. Gordon, an uncle
of Miss Clara Haralson, living in Lowndes County; Miss
Clara was there on a visit. She manifested pleasure at
meeting me, but there was evidence of pain mingled
with that expressed pleasure. This splendid woman was
sad but she said, "I cannot tell you how glad I am to see
you and how much I appreciate your visit, and especially when you had such a long walk from the station, that
we might see each other again after our mutual loss. I
know how much you were devoted to your noble

brother and his love for you was very great. Lieutenant Cater was worthy of the love we both felt for him. He was so learned, so noble, so grand and so devoted to his country. You are not surprised that I should look up to him as my hero and my heart's own King."

I said, "Miss Clara, what you have said and the vows I know were made by each of you, draws you very close to me. I shall always love you. I have only an hour to spend with you, as I must catch the next train for Montgomery. We must put away our sorrows and awake to the realities of the life before us. I wish I could stay longer with you, but my leave of absence has already expired and I must return to the army." We talked an hour or more and had much to tell about. Then I turned my footsteps towards the railroad. It was our last meeting.

CHAPTER XXXI

SPANISH FORT — LAST BATTLE — SURRENDER

On March 20th our brigade marched to Dog River Factory. The rain fell continuously all night. There was heavy cannonading on the Mobile Bay. The enemy's gunboats were in the bay which caused much excitement in the city. We returned to our camp on the 21st. On the 23d we crossed the bay in steamboats landing at Blakely. We bivouacked near Spanish Fort. On the 24th we moved six or seven miles from the fort and bivouacked near the bay. On the 25th we made a retrograde movement and camped a half mile from the fort. On the 26th we took position in the breastworks. We were surrounded by the enemy. We drove their pickets to their main line and returned to the breastworks. Heavy cannonading and skirmishing occurred on the 27th. The enemy continued their advance, entrenching at night until they were in talking distance. Cannonading and skirmishing continued for the next six days. A number of our men were killed or wounded. Steamboats could not come to the fort without very great risk because the enemy's batteries were planted on the beach near the main channel and our wounded were carried at night in canoes and yawls as far as Battery Eugee, where they were put on steamboats and carried to the city. We had a small division under the command of our brigade commander General Randall L. Gibson. The Fourteenth Texas Regiment, a regiment of Alabama troops, one of Georgia and one from North Carolina, added to our brigade (now only three regiments and very small) composed this division. It was too small to prevent the enemy from taking Spanish Fort. The cannonading on April 4th was the heaviest I had heard at this place. We lost one man killed and one wounded. On the 8th heavy cannonading was followed by a charge of the enemy, which turned our left and caused our evacuation of Spanish Fort that night. We came out on a treadway of two planks covered with moss to prevent the enemy from hearing us, to Battery Tracy, and there waited 'till daylight. We had to cross a marsh about one and a half miles the next morning, to where we could get on a steamboat which took us to the city. This marsh was soft mud and covered with reeds which had firm roots spread out, making a matting over the soft mud, beneath which it was bottomless. Only two or three men could step in one place before the matting would be broken, and when broken, woe to the man who placed the weight of his body on it. I have feared that some of our reported missing men were victims of that marsh.

The fear of capture at that stage of the war made us take risks we would not have done prior to Hood's loss of Georgia and Tennessee. During the last few days in Spanish Fort, the lines of the Federals were so close that we could talk to them. One day a soldier put his hat on a ramrod and held it above the top of the breastworks where the enemy could see it. A voice came, "Put your head in that hat if you want us to shoot at it." Mr. Baker, of our company, was killed in the breastworks where he thought he was safe. A minnieball came through a knothole in a plank which was used in making the works stronger, and struck him in the head, killing him instantly. There were men left on picket duty in the trenches when we left the fort. This seemed hard, but the commander had to do this, otherwise we would all have been captured.

The enemy took Blakely on the 9th and we knew that Mobile would be occupied by Federals very soon. We left there on the 11th, but before I got on the cars I went to see Miss Addie LeBaron, who, with her father and family, returned to their home in Mobile from Pollard when our regiment left that station in March 1863. Her father was loyal to our government to the end. He thought that the Confederate government would get a satisfactory settlement with the United States. He had very recently loaned $50,000 in gold to our government. We did not know that General Lee had surrendered in Virginia. Miss Addie said she hated to see us leave them in the hands of the Yankees and hoped we would soon return and force the Yankees to leave Mobile.

Our little army went from Mobile on the Mobile and Ohio Railroad, which was still in good condition. We left the cars at Meridian, Mississippi, and went into camp at that place. My work at Spanish Fort had been in the field hospital. I was present at the surgical operations and was sometimes called on to assist in dressing the wounds of our men.

Some of the Twentieth La. band had been captured at Nashville; some of mine had been killed and some of the Fourth La. band had shared the same fate. What was left of these bands, we gathered together at Mobile and we had a good band. B. Moses was the leader. After our little army had camped at Meridian, Gen. Gibson sent for me to come to his headquarters. When I reported to him he said, "Cater, I want you to take charge of our band; Moses deserted us at Mobile. We must have some music." I told the General that I had been changed so often that I concluded to remain with my company and not try the band service any more. He replied, "But I need you now for my band leader and will never allow you to be changed any more."

I thanked him and said, "I will do my best." There were sixteen members of the band and we commenced practice. Really, we didn't need Moses.

We left Meridian on April 22d and marched seven miles and went into camp. Here we got news of Gen. Lee's surrender of the Army of Northern Virginia to General Grant. We marched on the 23d and 24th and camped near Cuba Station on the Demopolis Railroad. Miss Augusta Evans, then a popular novelist, author of *Beulah*, *St. Elmo* and *Vashti*, was staying at a relative's in this neighborhood and Gen. Gibson said we must give her a serenade. This serenade was duly appreciated. She thanked us and asked the General to introduce her to each member of the band so that she could give us a good handshake to prove that she appreciated this honor. Our band made another serenade on May 5th, enjoyed a ride and had a good supper. This terminated my band career. It had been of short duration as a brigade band captain.

Mine was the last band of the Southern Confederacy. Gen. Dabney Maury was the man we had honored and he had received orders from Gen. Dick Taylor, the hero of the Mansfield, La. battle, and now commander of this department, to surrender this little Mobile army to General E. R. Canby, Federal commander of this department. On May 6th we had orders to go back to Meridian. We stacked arms there and waited for our paroles. Many men who had never seen any service and some who had quit on the change of commanders at Atlanta, were also at Meridian to receive paroles. Some of them were handled roughly by our soldiers, much to the amusement of the Federals who were guarding us.

I received my parole on the 17th. This was the end of my career as a Confederate soldier in the field, but there were some experiences yet to pass through, before I arrived home. Of course, I had to remain with the brigade until further disposition was made of us.

CHAPTER XXXII

IT IS OVER – GOING HOME

It was ordered that we receive transportation home. We took cars for Mobile, where we arrived the next morning and went into camp to await transportation to New Orleans. The city was filled with Federal soldiers and we were watched closely and had to be careful with words or actions. When marching to camp after leaving the cars we passed through a rough crowd of soldiers, most of whom seemed to be foreigners. One big fellow said, "The last damned one of them ought to be hanged." Of course no reply could be made to him. No doubt a majority of them felt that way towards us just then, and it was a foretaste of what was to follow if we, like the spaniel, "kissed the hand that smote us." At that time quiet submission was the only thing that could be done. Duty had called us to arms, and now duty called us home, and when there, we could take a survey of the situation and shape our course. I went to see some friends while the authorities were arranging for our transportation and enjoyed a nice dinner at a Mrs. McConnel's home. I was a guest at the home of Col. LeBaron in the evening in honor of some members of our regiment. I bade them good-bye, promising Miss Addie to visit her at some time in the future. I thought then that I could make the promise good, but unavoidably, it was never redeemed.

We took passage on the steamer *James Buttle* on the 17th en route for New Orleans, La., where we arrived

on the 18th of May. This city had fallen into the hands
of General B. F. Butler, who was remembered there as
"Beast Butler" for his cruelty, and as "Spoon Butler"
for having deprived the households of the city of every
piece of silverware, knives, forks, spoons, cups and
pitchers which had not been hurried out of reach of his
command. It seemed that there had been no objection
from those in authority at Washington to his line of
work when the prospects for final success became
brighter during the last years of the invasion. The cities
of Virginia offered a new field for this kind of work and
he was given command of a division in the Federal
armies over there. So he was not in New Orleans to
prevent the ladies from giving us a joyous welcome
when we entered the city. They were in line to cheer
us as we marched on the streets through the city.

We were on our way to the place prepared for our
reception, which was an enclosed cotton warehouse,
walled with brick and sheltered on the sides but open
for light and sunshine in the center. The entrance to
this place was, on this special occasion, guarded by
sentinels of the African persuasion: Augustus Ceazar
Cuffy on the right, and Washington Rastus Cuffy on the
left. They were armed with bright bayonetted muskets
which were brought strictly to 'carry arms' as we
entered, and brought to 'present arms' when his honor,
our pilot, Lieutenant Van Buren Cuffy, of the same
African persuasion, returned to make his exit after
placing us in our stations.

This is not an overdrawn picture. We were guarded
by Negro soldiers, some of whose former owners may

have been in our ranks in that prison, and this incident was only an index to the hearts of our successful enemies, and a foretaste of what was in store for us. The ladies of New Orleans were just as kind as it is possible for human beings to be. They brought us choice viands to eat, and various and sundry suits of clothing and hats to wear, so that if we desired to go out into the city, our guards would not say, "Halt dar, you can't go outen here, ceppin de cappen say so!" I declined making any changed in my garb, but many of our men accepted the clothes and hats, and when they had made the change and donned the hats, some of them stiff silk hats, making their appearance ludicrous, they would pass the sentinels unmolested. The guard knew, of course, and it was amusing to watch the expression on his face when one of these newly made civilians would pass out of the enclosure. But he had not received orders to halt anyone except the soldiers.

The Negro is naturally shrewd, and before Lincoln's invasion, his love and respect for the white man, and particularly the white children, was very great, and if he had been left to decide and act for himself after he was made a free man, and had not had wrong teaching by men in power during the Carpet Bag government in the South, his subsequent history would have been very different.

We were detained in New Orleans until our paroles could be countersigned. After this was accomplished we took passage at 6:00 P.M. on the steamer *Autocrat*, going north on the Mississippi River. We arrived at Baton Rouge at 10:00 P.M. on the 20th, and remained there the next day which was Sunday. We left that night at 10:00 P.M. and arrived at Natchez at 3:00 P.M. On the 23d we marched out to the park, rested an hour, and then moved down to the river. I met Theodore Bauer, a member of my band. He had come across the country from Meridian to Natchez instead of going with us to Mobile, but this was his home. I never knew why we were taken to Natchez. We left there on the same steamboat at 9 o'clock at night, going down the river as far as the mouth of the Red River, where we arrived at 6 o'clock the next morning. We started up Red River at 6:00 P.M. and arrived in Alexandria at 10:00 A.M. on the 26th. This was as far as our steamboat was going up Red River, so we had to leave it. The steamer, *Gus Hodges,* without a crew, was at the landing at this town and it was decided that we go on board and work our passage to Shreveport, Louisiana on it. Some of our men knew how to run an engine and some knew how to pilot. We made a pretty good run on the 27th. In the evening we had a reinforcement of engineers and pilots and concluded to run at night. We did pretty well until about midnight when the rudder of the boat, by some mismanagement, was broken; we could go no further. We could do nothing but wait until daylight. When morning came we found that we were at Bryant's Plantation. This was May 28th, 1865.

Here we separated. I have seen but few of the regiment since then. Some of them remained there until another steamboat came and took them to Shreveport. Some left to make their way across the country to their homes. With five of my company, I succeeded in finding Jordan's Ferry on Bayou Piere River and crossed there. I walked about twenty-five miles and stopped at night with an old man by the name of Rucker at Mrs. Ethridge's home. The others had taken different routes after we crossed Bayou Piere. My route led to Mansfield and I was making for that place! I resumed my journey the next morning, May 29th. I passed by the Moss plantation in which the most severe part of the Mansfield battle was fought. I didn't see any battle signs on the timber on the roadside. I arrived at Mansfield about 2:00 P.M. It was the same old town, and not much had changed since my boyhood school days there. I met an old schoolmate, Harry Draughn. I knew him but he did not recognize me, and I had to tell him who I was. He insisted on my going with him to his home. He wanted his mother and sister to see me. His father had died some years before. They expressed pleasure at seeing me again. They remembered me as a boy because I was often at their home. They soon prepared a nice dinner for me which I enjoyed, as I was very hungry! They said they were so glad to have me at their home again. I was in too great a hurry to stay any length of time after dinner, and proceeded on to Uncle John Greening's. He and his family treated me as though I were a 'returning prodigal.' My own home was yet twenty miles distant, and I told them that I must see my home folks before I slept again. Seeing that I could not be persuaded from continuing my journey, Uncle John ordered a horse saddled for me and told me I could return the horse and stay with him sometime later on. He gave me directions as to the roads and by 9:00

P.M. I was at the gate at home. My parents knew of the surrender and each passing day added to the suspense as they waited for my return. They knew I would come if living. My last letter to them was written at Mobile when our brigade was enroute to Spanish Fort, where the last fighting was done. They knew that Mobile had fallen but did not know my fate. They were watching and waiting. So many changes had taken place since I was with them.

I cannot tell of my own feelings as I dismounted at the gate and heard the 'faithful' watch dog's bay deep mouth welcome. I knew welcome awaited me, not as a returning prodigal, but as the only one left of the three this home had furnished as soldiers to the Confederate States army. I knew there would be joy, but with that joy would be sadness because my presence would bring recollections of those who did not return, and more vivid recollections just now. The family had not yet retired and the lamps in the house were giving light. As I stepped on the gallery my father and mother were coming to meet me, my oldest sister following. Of course they knew me; I was only a little older. In a few minutes the house Negroes wanted to, and did hug me. The Negroes at home had not bothered about freedom; that was something they had yet to learn about. They loved me and were glad I was home again, and that home heretofore their home. My career as a soldier was ended.

The Federal armies, as already shown, were successful; the soldiers returned to their homes in triumph and were satisfied. They found more pleasure in being freed from army duties, from army discipline, from the fear of whistling musket balls and bursting shells, than in rejoicing over the defeat of the southern soldiers. But not so the men and women who had aggravated the southern people to the extent that they, in the interests of peace and harmony, and in the exercise of their constitutional rights as American citizens, had withdrawn their allegiance to the United States government and formed a separate government. They said, "Victory is not enough—there must be some punishment for the survivors of the defeated armies. They must be humiliated. They must be made to see their former slaves placed in authority over them. They must see their intelligent Negroes put in places of honor in the districts, in the counties, in the halls of legislation. Social standing must be given to the Negroes!" Not a flattering outlook, but every jot and tittle true, and for the present we must be harmless as doves but wise as serpents.

I had been at home about two weeks when a company of Negro soldiers passed our home on their way to Logansport, a village on the Sabine River, the dividing line at that point between Louisiana and Texas, about five miles south of our home. Their captain was a white man. He was made provost marshal at Longansport and took control of affairs, both civil and military, not only of the town but surrounding country. The problem before us was to adjust ourselves to the new order of things and to be very careful as to the management of the Negroes at home and in the community. They were thrown upon their own resources without training or preparation of any kind for business. Mr. Lincoln's proclamation of January 1863, declaring them free, had been for a double purpose, the main one being to break up the Confederate armies, and force the soldiers to go home. But this did not become necessary because the Negroes paid no attention to it, except in cities and towns. And those who left home to go to the Federals were used in digging breastworks and put in front to protect white soldiers from the bullets of Confederate soldiers.

The Negroes needed good advice and wise counsel now. This made our responsibility very serious because, with freedom, came men to the South from states which knew nothing of Negro slavery. These men had false ideas and wrong views as to their condition (except in isolated cases where the law was violated). These men, instead of giving correct advice, endeavored to instill hatred in the Negroes' minds against their former owners and friends, and to impress the idea upon them that they were now equal in all respects to the southern white people. These teachings caused much trouble and in some parts of our country, much bloodshed. It was several years before the Negroes learned that they had been duped and used only for pecuniary advantage by those men who had justly earned the name Carpet Baggers. These men had assistance from scalawags. The Carpet Baggers were from the northern states and the scalawags were natives or residents of the southern states before the Lincoln invasion. This Carpet Bagger rule finally became so unreasonable and so unjust, with the continued effort to control the southern states in defiance of law and the principles of justice, that it resulted in secret organizations for self protection. These organizations were of greater proportions than was ever known. They had a name, and 'tis true there were some excesses at times, but these were never approved and on the contrary, severely condemned. The fact remained that this was our country and the determination was to bring order out of confusion and to rebuild our homes.

After the company of Negro soldiers was stationed at Logansport, my father asked me to call our Negroes together and speak to them of the new condition of our country. He asked me to say to them that they had heretofore worked for us and had been true and faithful servants, but now they were free and must depend on themselves and do the best they could. They had a warm place in our hearts and we would never forget them. Our advice would be for them to remain at home for the balance of the year (1865) and continue the cultivation of the growing crop and gather it in the fall of the year as they had always done, and that half of it would belong to them. After that time they could make arrangements to suit themselves.

I carried out Father's instructions fully, and told them of how much pleasure it gave me when I remembered my spending many Sabbath evenings with them when a boy, teaching some of them to read, and reading to them from the Bible and other books. This was one of the causes of their esteem for me. They agreed to Father's proposition and returned to their 'quarters.' They did not leave us until after the end of the year.

This situation of affairs at home gave me a long vacation.

It was not really necessary for me to work at home and there seemed to be a desire among the homefolks for me to remain with them the balance of that year. Father still loved to take an occasional drive for deer. We hunted some; I spent some pleasant days with relatives in and near Mansfield; made several visits to Keachie, and was with associates of school days there.

But these pleasures were not sufficient to satisfy me. Instead of continuing as a music teacher I decided to take up medicine. The changed condition of our country made the outlook gloomy for my former profession, but there would always be work for the doctor. I commenced reading anatomy and physiology with a view of advancing to chemistry and the study of diseases and their treatment, and attending the medical courses in New Orleans or Mobile later. There was nothing in sight to promise the means necessary to complete this course, and it was really necessary for me to be at home during their present conditions of our country. I knew the time I devoted to this study would be beneficial to me, even if disappointed in securing a complete preparation for that kind of work.

CHAPTER XXXIII

AFTER THE WAR — RETURN TO TEXAS

In our vicinity there was quiet and peace, and we paid no attention (except to watch them) to the Captain and his company at Logansport. A similar outfit was at Mansfield. They opened the jail doors there and liberated the violators of law who were in prison. Among them was a horse thief whom my father had followed three days alone into Texas before overtaking him, and had brought him back on the horse he had stolen from father's horse lot.

In October I found that in addition to study and pastimes, there was an inclination to visit Texas and shake hands with my old comrades of the Third Texas Cavalry who had returned home and were living in Henderson and Rusk. But that was only a minor part of that inclination. I really wanted to see the author of the many appreciated letters which had found their way to me in the army, and whose hands had knit the woolen socks which, by wearing one pair over my boots and the other pair over my ears, had prevented my feet and ears from being frozen on the snow covered prairies in the Indian Territory in December, 1861.

The October mornings were bringing forecasts of expected frosts. The dew on the grass in the sun's rays sparkled almost like frost. My gray uniform, which had been laid aside when I came home, was still intact, and was again called into requisition. Not that there was disloyalty lurking in me, but because it was comfortable and I could find nothing in the stores that I wanted. My father had given me a beautiful horse when I came home. Uncle Bob, the oldest Negro man on the place, who had been too old for several years to do any field work, said he was saving that horse for me, and had brushed and rubbed him until his hair was glossy. My sister had named him Rosenante because when Father bought him he was so poor she said he resembled Don Quixote's charger of that name.

Taking a shotgun with me for company, I mounted Rosenante early one morning, and set out for Texas. The counties of Shelby and Rusk, through which my route led, were not densely populated and there was an abundance of game, but my errand was not to kill turkeys or deer, although there were several opportunities when I could have used my gun to bring down a buck whose antlers reminded me of a chair on his head. My first night was spent at the home of a Mr. Carraway in Shelby County. He was a successful farmer whose grain bins were filled to overflowing and Rosenante fared sumptuously while Mr. Carraway's table at both supper and breakfast was furnished with such viands as to tempt a young man with a good appetite to decide to be a farmer. The armies of Phil Sheridan and Tecumseh Sherman had not been in this part of the country and the torch had not been applied to the residences, barns and smoke houses of the people. They were pursuing the even tenor of their way, unmolested and seemingly undisturbed about the changed condition in our southern states. My second day's ride brought me to the home of the cause of this Texas visit.

This trip to Texas ends this history of a private soldier in the Lincoln war. This war was unjust and unnecessary. Personal ownership of slaves could have and should have been ended without the sword and musket, which caused so much sorrow and suffering, devastation and bloodshed. National questions demand fair consideration, but in this case we must conclude that personal ambition prevented it. Some references to Gen. Joseph E. Johnston and other facts worth remembering as gathered from scraps of information and statements by others are in the following pages.

D. J. CATER

TRIBUTE TO A GREAT GENERAL

By Douglas John Cater

Some references to General Joseph E. Johnston: Born in Cherry Grove, Virginia February 3, 1807. Graduated at the United States Military Academy in 1829. Was in the Florida and Mexican Wars. Was promoted to Quartermaster General of the United States Army with the rank of brigadier general in June, 1860. Resigned his commission when Virginia seceded from the United States and offered his services to his native state. The governor of Virginia made him Major General of the Virginia Volunteers.

Then, President Davis made him a brigadier general in the Confederate States army, the highest office in the army at that time. His time was then devoted to the organization and training of the volunteers who composed the Army of Northern Virginia. Think of the work required to make soldiers of these citizens from the various walks of peaceful life: preachers, lawyers, doctors, merchants, clerks, farmers, blacksmiths, bookkeepers, mechanics, etc., many of them bringing servants for cooks, ostlers, and other camp duties; with trunks of clothing and other baggage, all to be provided for and the men to be fed. He was equal to the emergency and subsequent Department of the Army of Virginia. Actions proved how well his work was done.

At the Battle of Manassas (or Bull Run), Gen.

Beauregard was managing the Confederate forces so well against the Federal armies of Generals Patterson, McDowell and McClellan, that Gen. Johnston, although commander-in-chief, made no change of plans except to lead a charge, carrying the flag of the 4th Alabama regiment to victory. The fruits of this victory added to the Confederacy 28 cannons, 4,500 muskets, 500,000 cartridges, 64 artillery horses and harness, 26 wagons and camp equipage, clothing and other military property.

General Johnston was censured by some critics for not following up this victory by a capture of the city of Washington, but he was always opposed to northern invasion and believed successful defense should be our policy.

The Confederate secretary of war, Judah P. Benjamin, was a source of much annoyance to him, and this continued annoyance caused Stonewall Jackson to prepare papers of resignation from the army; but General Johnston succeeded in convincing Jackson that his resignation would be too great a loss to the army. At that time the president had no ill feeling towards General Johnston and yielded to his wishes and removed Mr. Benjamin.

When the capitol, Richmond, Virginia, was threatened, Gen. Johnston proposed an attack on McClellan's army in front of Richmond to prevent a siege, but in this, he was opposed by Gen. Robert E. Lee and the president agreed with Gen. Lee. The movements of the army following this decision brought on much heavy fighting and the Battle of "Seven Pines" was a conclusion of several days of severe but successful battles. General Johnston was slightly wounded in the right shoulder by a musket ball, and a few moments afterwards was unhorsed by a heavy fragment of shell which struck his breast. Darkness terminated this battle. The president visited him, manifesting sympathy and friendship, but the next day the president placed Gen. Robert E. Lee in command of the Army of Virginia, and he returned with the army to camp near Richmond.

The president sanctioned or agreed to a changed law which placed Gen. Joseph E. Johnston fourth in rank instead of first, and Johnston wrote a letter to him complaining of this injustice. The president was so angered by this letter that he never forgave him. This was shown afterwards when Johnston was in command of the army and the Department of Tennessee.

Grant, with an army flushed with victory, expected to overwhelm and capture Johnston and his little army at Jackson. But Grant was afraid of Johnston and of coming near Jackson, so he stopped to build breastworks and lay siege to Jackson. After a few days he assaulted Johnston but was repulsed with severe loss. Johnston did not lose any men. He notified the president that it was unsafe to try to hold Jackson because it was too easy to be flanked. After moving all government supplies to safety he evacuated the place, much to the surprise of General Grant. His removal from the command followed this action.

After Gen. Bragg's complete rout at Missionary Ridge with a heavy loss of men and material and a retreat to Dalton, Georgia, Gen. Johnston was returned to the command of the army and Department of Tennessee. He found the little army poorly clad, poorly fed and smarting under defeat, but his coming brought great joy to the soldiers. There was a magnetism about this great man which gave love and confidence to his soldiers. They knew that he was careless of his own blood, but that he was careful of that of his men, that he knew when to take them under fire and how to bring them out. The winter soon passed; his men were rested, well clothed, well fed and ready to do cheerfully what he told them. I am writing this not from 'hearsay,' because I was a private soldier in the army at Dalton, and I want the world to know the truth about General Joseph E. Johnston.

When May, 1864 came, Gen. Sherman, commanding an army of 110,000 Federal soldiers, struck Dalton. When Johnston was removed from command at Atlanta on July 17, 1864, Sherman's strength was 70,000 men. Where were the 40,000 which made up the 110,000? They were lost between Dalton and Atlanta: a fearful answer to the charges brought against Gen. Johnston, that he would not fight, that he would not defend Atlanta, that he disregarded the president's instructions. He found 36,000 men at Dalton December 20, 1863. He had 41,000 men in May, 1864 to face Sherman's 110,000 well armed and well equipped soldiers. And with this difference the president was disappointed because Sherman was not driven out of Georgia!

I learned when still in Atlanta, that while at Jonesboro, before leaving for his home, Gen. Johnston called together some old men and boys and successfully turned back a raid of Federal cavalry which had gotten in the rear of Hood's army. This only proved his great love for, and true loyalty to his country, notwithstanding the treatment he had received from the authorities at Richmond.

Some writer said that when Gen. Sherman got news of the change in commanders, he said, "Heretofore the fighting has been as Johnston pleased; now it will be as I please." The army of Tennessee heard the shouts of the Federals when they learned that Gen. Hood and not Gen. Johnston confronted them. After Gen. Hood escaped with a fragment of his army from Tennessee, Gen. Robert E. Lee, commander-in-chief of all the Confederate forces, ordered Johnston to come back to his shattered army and prevent Sherman's victorious army from joining Gen. Grant in Virginia. The president made no objection. He had learned that Johnston made no mistakes. Johnston's country was first with him and he obeyed Gen. Lee's order.

In the closing days, the greatness, the nobleness and the splendid characteristics of this grand man were made manifest. After getting news of Gen. Lee's surrender he did not surrender but succeeded in making terms of peace with General Sherman: that the war should end, the soldiers be paroled and have transportation home. He paid his soldiers $39,000 in silver which he had orders to send to the president. He asked that the great amount of coin in the president's hands be paid to the soldiers, but never received an answer to his request. Here is his last order to his army:

"Comrades, in terminating our official relations I earnestly exhort you to observe faithfully the terms of pacification agreed upon, and to discharge the obligations of good and peaceful citizens as well as you have performed the duties of thorough soldiers in the field. By such a course you will best secure the comfort of your families and kindred and restore tranquility to our country. You will return to your homes with the admiration of our people, won by the courage and noble devotion you have displayed in this long war. I shall always remember with pride the loyal support and generous confidence you have given me. I now part with you with deep regret and bid you farewell with feelings of cordial friendship and with earnest wishes that you may have hereafter all the prosperity and happiness to be found in the world."

J.E. Johnston - General

INDEX

Adams, Gen. Dan, 135, 136, 148, 156, 164, 174
Adams, Dood, 43, 44
Adams, E. B. "Ned", 37, 39, 41-46
Adams, Elisha, 37
Adams, Frank, 43
Adams, Leah Cater, 37
Adams, Sam, 37, 39
Adams, Tom, 37, 39, 44-46
Adams, William, 44
Alabama, 1, 158, 160, 171, 177, 205
Alexander's Bridge, Va., 160
Alexandria, La., 216
Alston, Emma, 52
Alston, Tempie, 52
Alto, Tex., 54-56
Angelina Co., Tex., 45
Arkansas River, 79, 82, 83, 99, 126
Armstrong, Capt., 116
Armstrong, Col., 82
Armstrong, Frank, 85
Armstrong, Jim, 72
Army of the Tennessee, 126
Army of the West, 112
Atlanta, Ga., 147, 171, 181-184, 188-192, 199
Autocrat (steamer), 215

Baker, Mr., 209
Baker's Creek, Battle of, 153

Baldwin, W. O., 39
Baptist Assoc. of N. Louisi-ana, 26
Barker, Jim, 107, 108, 132, 135
Barton, Matt, 84
Bate's Division, 181, 202
Baton Rouge, La., 215
Battery Eugee, 208
Battery Tracy, 209
Bauer, Theodore, 192, 216
Bayou Piere River, La., 217
Bear Creek (Ala.), 204
Beauregard, Gen. P.G.T., 67, 69, 126, 130, 137
Beech Grove, Tenn., 148
Belleville, Ala., 205
Bentonville, Ark., 112
Big Black River, 182
Big Cedar River, 194
Big Frog Bayou (Ark.), 99, 109, 110, 113
Black Republican Party, 58, 68
Blakely, Ala., 208, 210
Boggess, Giles S., 72, 101, 132
Bolton, Miss., 152-154
Bonham, John, 142,143
Braden, Mr., 162, 176
Bragg, Gen. Braxton, 126, 130, 136-138, 145, 149, 158, 164-168, 184, 186
Brandon, Miss., 157
Breckinridge, Gen. John C., 148
Breckinridge's Division, 158, 159

Bridgeport, Ala., 158
Broughton, Ben, 151
Brown, John Henry, 85
Brown, Taylor, 114, 115, 132
Brown, Wesley, 2
Bryant's Plantation, 216
Buckner, Gen. Simon B., 158
Buford, Gen. Abraham, 203
Burnsville, Miss., 204
Burnt Corn, Ala., 141, 144, 172, 205
Butler, Maj., 144, 162
Butler, Gen. Benjamin F., 214

Cabell, Gen. William L., 131
Campbell, Mrs., 13
Canby, Gen. E. R. S., 212
Carlton, Sallie, 30
Carraway, Mr., 224
Cartersville, Ga., 181
Carthage, Mo., 95, 96
Cary, Fannie, 173, 174
Cary, John D., 144, 173
Cary, Kate, 144, 173 ,174
Cassville, Ark., 83
Castor Bayou (La.), 20
Cater, E. Lawrence, 26, 141, 144, 172, 174, 205, 206
Cater, Edwin, 6, 141
Cater, Fannie, 172, 205, 206
Cater, Junius, 192
Cater, Kate, 6
Cater, Martha, 6
Cater, Ned, 172
Cater, Rufus, 2, 3, 6, 18, 19, 26, 27, 46, 60, 128, 135, 138, 142, 147-151, 155-164, 207
Cater, Tom, 6

Cater, Victoria, 2, 6, 24, 26, 27, 192
Cater, Wade, 1-11, 22-25, 32-35, 46, 60, 139, 150
Cave Springs, Ga., 194
Cedar Town, Ga., 194
Chalmers, Gen. James R., 202, 203
Chattahoochee River, 183, 194
Chattanooga, Tenn., 147, 150, 158, 162, 164
Cheatham, Gen. Benjamin F., 188, 200
Cheatham's Division, 160, 183
Cherokee Co., Ala., 194
Cherokee Co., Tex., 62
Cherokee Indians, 100
Cherokee Nation, I. T., 104, 105
Chickamauga, Battle of, 160-163, 174, 176, 179
Chickamauga Creek (Ga.), 159, 167
Chickasaw Indians, 100
Chickasaw Nation, I. T., 77-79, 94
Childress, Rufus, 132
Chilton, George W., 77
Chisholm, Capt., 88
Choctaw Nation, I. T., 77-79, 94
Choctaw Indians, 100, 105
Churchill's Arkansas Cavalry Regt., 85, 116
Chustenahlah, Battle of, 104, 112
Cleburne, Gen. Pat, 188, 201
Cleburne's Division, 180, 183
Cleveland, Ala., 195
Clinton, Miss., 152
Collin Co., Tex., 77

Collins, Malvern, 161
Columbia, Tenn., 196, 200, 203
Comanche Indians, 100
Conecuh Co., Ala., 141
Conway, A., 21, 22, 25
Conway, Con, 169
Cooper, Col., 100-105, 154, 157
Coosa River, Ala., 194, 195
Corinth, Miss., 127-132, 135
Courtland, Ala., 195
Creek Indians, 100
Crockett, Tex., 38
Crosby, Erastus "Ratt", 30
Cross Hollows, Ark., 111
Cuba Station, Miss., 211
Cumberland Gap, Tenn., 158
Crump's Battalion, 96
Cumby, Capt. R. S., 72, 81, 82,
    91, 94, 98, 121, 127, 132
Curtis, Gen. Samuel R., 111,
    112, 115, 120

Dallas, Ga., 194
Dallas, Tex., 77,82
Dalton, Ga., 167-182
Daniels, Lt. Frank, 107,108
Davis, Jefferson, 64, 65, 149,
    165, 182, 186
Demopolis Railroad, 211
Department of Tennessee, 184,
    205
Department of the West, 149
De Soto Parish, La., 7, 21, 30, 55
Desplooce, Mr., 172
Dickson, Miss, 152
Dillon, Major, 85
Dog River Factory, Ala., 208
Draughn, Harry, 217

Drew, Col., 105
Duck River, Tenn., 147, 200, 203
Durham, Dock, 72, 104, 105
Duvall's Bluff, Ark., 126

East Point, Ga., 191
Ector, Jennie, 191
Ector, M. D., 72, 77, 93, 100,
    106, 131, 191
Ector's Brigade, 202
Egypt, Miss., 205
Elk Horn Tavern, Battle of, 111
Elysian Fields, Tex., 5, 48
Embry's Arkansas Cavalry
    Regt., 112, 116
Escambia River (Ala.), 145
Ethridge, Mrs., 217
Evans, Augusta, 211
Evergreen, Ala., 144, 172, 205

Farmington, Battle of, 134
Fayetteville, Ark., 82, 83, 97, 98,
    111
Fayetteville, Ga., 193
Finch, Mrs., 206
Florence, Ala., 196, 204
Forrest, Gen. Nathan B., 160,
    198, 200-203
Forsyth, Ga., 191
Fort Gibson, I. T., 101, 102
Fort Smith, Ark., 77, 82, 105
Fort Sumter, S.C., 67, 69
Fourteenth Texas Regiment, 208
Fourth Kentucky Inf. Regt., 148
Fourth Louisiana Band, 192, 210
Fourth La. Inf. Regt., 202
Franklin, Tenn., 200
Franklin, Battle of, 200, 201

Franks, Jack, 162
Frazier, Judge, 65
Fremont, Gen., 96

Gadsden, Ala., 195
Garrett, John, 18, 19
Gayle, Matt, 140
Gibson, Gen. Randall L., 203, 208, 211
Godfrey, Dr., 17
Good's Texas Battery, 96
Gordon, Mr., 206
Gordon, Miss Bamma, 143
Gordon, Miss Daught, 143
Gordon, Miss Tennie, 143
Grand Cane, La., 18, 19, 27
Grant, Gen. U. S., 129, 131, 149, 152-157, 165-168, 193
Graves, Capt. Y. W., 40, 41
Grayson Co., Tex., 77
Green, Judge, 141, 144
Green Co., Mo., 92
Greening, Frank, 32-36
Greening, John, 21, 56, 217
Greening, Dr. Wade, 32
Greer, Elkanah, 72, 82, 113-120
Greer's Regiment, 82
Griffin, Ga., 190
Gus Hodges (vessel), 216
Guy, Gus, 56
Guy, Sam, 56

Hall, Tom, 30, 31
Handley, Capt., 144,162
Haralson, Clara, 143, 160, 206, 207
Haralson, Judge John B., 143
Hardee, Gen. W. J., 137, 188

Hardee's Corps, 191, 192
Harney, Gen. W. S., 86
Harrison Co., Tex., 5, 48, 174
Hebert, Col., 85, 117, 120
Helm, Gen., 148
Henderson, Tex., 58-75, 81, 92, 99, 183, 223
Hendrick, Dr. Gus, 164
Hendrick, Matt, 162
Hendricks, Tom, 8, 15
Henryville, Tenn., 197
Hinson, Mr., 162
Hodges, Capt., 151
Hogg, Gen. Joseph L., 59, 77, 131
Hollingsworth, Dick, 49
Honey, Sam, 113, 115
Hood, Gen. John B., 179, 183, 184, 188-194, 200-202
Hood's Divison, 160
Hoover's Gap, Tenn., 148
Houston, Sam, 64
Houston Co., Tex., 38
Hunnicutt's Spring, Tex., 76, 77
Huntsville, Tex., 37-39
Huntsville Penitentiary, 38, 39, 73

Iron Mountain, Tex., 92
Isham, Bill, 101, 109, 113, 115
Iuka, Miss., 204
Ivey, Henry, 143, 144, 160

Jackson, Governor (Missouri), 96
Jackson, Miss., 149-154, 157, 158, 167
Jacksonville, Ala., 194

James Buttle (vessel), 213
Jayhawkers, 96, 98
Johnson, Capt., 97
Johnston, Gen. Albert Sydney, 130
Johnston, Gen. Joseph E., 149, 152-158, 168, 169, 176-186, 226-231
Jones' Division, 137
Jonesborough, Ga., 191, 192
Jordan's Ferry, 217

Kansas, 95
Kauffman Co., Tex., 76
Keachie, La., 21, 24, 25, 31, 45-49, 52, 60, 128, 169, 222
Kelly, Mr., 64
Kelly, Lewis, 97, 98
Kenesaw Mountain, Ga., Battle of, 180
Kingston, Ga., 179
Kingston School (De Soto Parish, La.), 30, 36
Knoxville, Tenn., 158, 165

Lafayette, Ga., 158
Lafitte, Ramy, 165
Lake Ponchartrain (La.), 3
Lane, Walter P., 77, 95, 113, 134, 135
Lavaca Co., Tex., 37
LeBaron, Mr., 143, 210, 213
LeBaron, Addie, 143, 144, 210, 213
Lee, Mr., 19
Lee, Gen. Robert E., 159, 165, 168, 179,193 ,210
Lee, Gen. Stephen D., 186, 188, 203
Lee's Corps, 191
Lethatchie Station, Ala., 206
Lewis, Mr., 39, 40
Lincoln, Abraham, 59, 65, 86, 220
Line Creek (Miss.), 157
Lockhart, Bob, 41
Logansport, La., 19, 20, 46, 219, 221, 223
Lomax, L. L., 85
Lone Star Defenders, 59, 77
Longstreet, Gen. James, 158, 161
Longstreet's Corps, 158, 160, 165, 166
Lookout Mountain, 165-167
Lost Mountain, Ga., 194
Lovejoy Station, Ga., 192
Lowndes Co., Ala., 143, 206
Lyon, Gen., 77, 80, 87-89, 94, 95

M. & A. Railroad, 193
Mabry, Capt., 97, 132, 134
Macon, Ga., 21
McConnel, Mrs., 213
McCormick, Isabella, 29, 30
McCormick, John, 171
McCulloch, Gen. Ben, 81, 85, 87, 89, 96, 100, 111-119, 130
McDugald, Dr. Wallace, 131
McIntosh, Gen. James, 85, 100-105, 112, 115-119, 130
McKinney, Tex., 77
McNair's Regiment, 111, 116
McPherson, Gen., 178
McPherson, Elizabeth, 144, 172
McRea's Regiment, 111, 116

McVoy, Bella, 174
McVoy, Charley, 174
McVoy, Kate Cater, 174
McVoy, Tennie, 174
Mansfield, La., 7, 13, 15, 20, 23, 47, 56, 181, 212, 217, 222, 223
Marietta, Ga., 181, 190, 194
Marshall, Sam, 75, 84, 123
Marshall, Rev. W. K., 63, 73, 75
Marshall, Tex., 52, 65, 141
Mason's *Sacred Harp* (book), 27
Masonic Institute (Henderson,Tex.), 58, 59, 62, 66
Mathis, Mr., 56
Maury, Dabney, 120, 121, 202, 211
Memphis, Tenn., 126-128
Memphis & Charleston Railroad, 195, 204
Meridian, Miss., 150, 210-212
Meyers, Matt, 91, 92
Miller, Henry, 103, 105
Milton, Fla., 26, 32, 141
Missionary Ridge, Tenn., 165
Missionary Ridge, Battle of, 167-169
Mississippi River, 4, 176, 182, 191, 215
Missouri, 77, 82, 83, 86, 87, 91, 96, 98
Miszner, J. C., 59, 61
Mitchell, Prof. John B., 47, 50, 53, 58, 59, 62, 63, 70, 73, 135
Mitchell's Cavalry Regt., 111, 116
Mobile, Ala., 3, 140-143, 150, 205, 208, 210-213, 218
Mobile and Ohio R.R., 210

Mobile Camp, Ala., 145
Mobile *Register* (newspaper), 145
Montgomery, Gen., 95
Montgomery, Maj., 85
Montgomery, Ala., 3, 140, 146, 147, 150, 174
Moore, Joe, 192
Mortin Station, Miss., 157, 158
Moscow, Tex., 39, 41, 44
Moses, B., 211
Moss Plantation (La.), 217
Mount Pleasant, Tenn., 197

Nacogdoches, Tex., 45
Nacogdoches Co., Tex., 45
Nashville, Tenn., 193, 195, 198-203
Natchez, Miss., 216
Neosho, Mo., 96
Nevill's Prairie, Tex., 38
New Orleans, La., 3, 4, 6, 26, 157, 213-215
New Salem, Tex., 136
New Sparta, Ala., 174
Newman, Arthur, 187
Nineteenth Louisiana Infan-try Regt., 128, 132, 135-213
Ninth Texas Cavalry Regt., 100

Oak Hills, Mo., 90, 91
Okolona, Miss., 205
Old Stone Fort (Nacogdoches), 45
Opelika, Ala., 171
Opothleyohola (Creek Chief), 100, 105
Oristenola River (Ga.), 179

Palmetto, Ga., 193,194
Pea Ridge, Battle of, 111-119, 130
Peachtree Creek, Ga., 185
Pearl River (Miss.), 155
Pearson, Capt. N. G., 144, 181
Pegues, Fannie, 56
Pegues, Lizzie, 56
Pemberton, Gen. John C., 149-153
Pensacola, Fla., 140, 145
Philson, Dr., 195, 196
Pike, Gen. Albert, 112, 116-118
Pillow, Gen., 197
Pine Mountain, Ga., 181
Pineville, Mo., 95
Pleasant Hill, La., 21
Poe, Foster, 44
Poe, Willis, 134
Polk, Gen. Leonidas, 159, 161, 181, 197
Polk's Corps, 159, 160
Polk Co., Tex., 27, 37, 39, 43, 45
Pollard, Ala., 140-145, 172, 210
Powell, Lt., 191, 193
Powell, Wesley, 171
Price, Gen. Sterling, 77, 82-90, 96, 111, 115, 118, 120, 130-135
Prude, Sgt., 144, 151
Pulaski, Tenn., 203
Pulaski, Tex., 38

Rains, Dr. C. B., 51
Rambin, Volsey, 28
Reagan, Miss Em, 62, 63, 66, 73-75, 92, 100, 136, 177, 191, 192
Rector's Cavalry Regt., 111, 116
Red River, 4, 78, 216

Resaca, Ga., 178, 179
Rienzi, Miss., 204
Ringgold, Ga., 158
Rochelle, Dr., 35
Rome, Ga., 158
Rorrison, A. C., 75, 76, 80, 81, 84, 87-102, 110, 122, 124, 131, 132, 182, 183
Rosecrans Army, 158, 162, 164, 165
Roy, Professor, 30-32, 36
Rucker, Mr., 217
Rusk, Tex., 50-52, 58, 60, 62, 77, 131, 223
Rusk Co., Tex., 64, 66, 94, 136, 192, 224

Sabine River, 19, 38, 219
St. Charles Hotel (New Orleans), 4
Saltillo, Miss., 204
San Antonio, Tex., 77
Sand Mountain, Ala., 195
Santro, Ala., 194
Schofield, Gen., 178
Selma, Ala., 146
Seminole Indians, 100
Seventh Texas Cavalry Regt., 96
Shelby Co., Tex., 46, 224
Sherman, Gen. W. T., 165, 168, 171, 178-183,193-195, 199
Sherman, Tex., 77
Shiloh, Tenn., 130
Shoal Creek (Tenn.), 203, 204
Shreveport, La., 4-6, 30 ,216
Sigel, Gen. Franz, 88-90, 111-115, 120
Simms, Col., 102-105

Simms' Regiment, 100, 112
Slocumb, Capt., 155
Slocumb's Battery, 155-157
Smith, Capt., 191
Smith, Frank, 142, 168
Smith Co., Tex., 76
Snake Creek Gap (Ga.), 179
Snodgrass Hill, 162
Spanish Fort, Ala., 208-210
Sparta, Ala., 141, 144, 173
Spilker, Mr., 47
Springfield, Mo., 83, 93, 96, 97
Spring Hill, Tenn., 200
Springs, Miss., 152
Stephens, Alexander, 64
Stevenson, Gen. Carter L., 203
Stevenson, Ala., 158
Stewart, Gen., 188
Stewart's Division, 160
Stone's Regiment, 96, 112
Stovall's Brigade, 202
Sturgis, Ed., 75, 84
Sulphur Springs, Tex., 93
Summerville, Ala., 195

Tallahassee, Fla., 144
Taylor, Miss Ella, 27, 29
Taylor, Frank, 77
Taylor, Gen. Richard, 212
Tennessee River, 158, 164, 166,
    193, 196, 197, 202, 204
Tensas Landing, 150
Third Louisana Infantry Regt.,
    85, 88, 111, 117, 120
Third Texas Cavalry Regt., 77,
    82, 85, 116, 128, 131, 135, 181,
    182, 223
Thirtieth La. Inf. Regt., 202

Thomas, Fanny, 29
Thomas, Gen. George C., 178,
    195
Thompson Hotel (Rusk, Tex.),
    50, 62
Tinnon, Professor, 55
Tomlinson, Mrs., 172
Tomlinson, Augusta, 172
Tomlinson, Isadore, 172
Trinity River (Tex.), 38, 76
Tucker, Gen., 203
Tullahoma, Tenn., 147
Tupelo, Miss., 135, 136, 140,
    182, 204, 205
Turner, Ben, 121
Turner, Col. R. W., 174, 187,
    190, 195
Twentieth Louisiana Band, 177,
    210
Twenty-Seventh Louisiana In-
    fantry Regt., 150

U. S. & T. Railroad, 152

Van Buren, Ark., 99, 106
Van Dorn, Gen. Earl, 112, 115,
    117, 119, 120, 130, 205
Van Wort, Ga., 194
Van Zandt Co., Tex., 76
Vicksburg, Miss., 139, 149-153

Walker Co., Tex., 37
Walker's Division, 160
Warren River, Ala., 195
Wartrace, Tenn., 147, 150
Washington Artillery, 157
Watson, Charley, 82
Waverly, Tex., 39

Wells, Fannie, 30
West Point, Miss., 150, 205
Western Army, the, 126
Wheeler, Gen. Joseph, 160, 179, 181
White River (Ark.), 126
Whitesides, John, 75, 84
Whitfield's Texas Battalion of Cavalry, 96, 116
Williams, Lt., 162
Williams, Joe, 47, 169
Williams, Margarette, 47
Willis, Dr., 27

Wilson's Creek, Battle of, 86-90, 91, 94, 96
Winans, Col., 141-145, 151, 167, 174, 175
Winchester, Lou, 127, 128
Wiser's Ferry, 38
Womack, Mrs. Catherine, 44
Womack, Nellie, 44
Wynne, Jessee, 132, 134

Young's Regiment of Cavalry, 96, 111, 112
Ypsilanti, Mich., 76